VOLUME 1

TMD **Publishing**

PODCASTS.
BOOKS.
FILMS.
SEMINARS.
COACHING.

thatsmydadproject.com

BREAKING CYCLES OF
GENERATIONAL FATHERLESSNESS
AND INSPIRING FATHERS
TO BECOME GREAT DADS

Dad Stories
63 True Stories That Will Inspire You To Be A Great Dad.
Volume 1.

Copyright
© 2023 by That's My Dad Project
Published by TMD Publishing

All rights reserved. No part of this publication may be reproduced, distributed, or transmitted in any form or by any means, including photocopying, recording, or other electronic or mechanical methods, without the prior written permission of the publisher, except in the case of brief quotations embodied in critical reviews and certain other noncommercial uses permitted by copyright law.

ISBN: 978-1-959083-04-7 (Hardcover)
ISBN: 978-1-959083-05-4 (Paperback)
ISBN: 978-1-959083-06-1 (eBook)
ISBN: 978-1-959083-07-8 (Audiobook)

Cover artwork by Colin Edwards.
Book formatting & design by Colin Edwards.

First printing edition 2023.
Printed in the USA.

www.thatsmydadproject.com

DISCLAIMER
Names of individuals, places, and organizations as well as identifying characteristics and details have been changed when necessary to protect privary.

CREDITS

Founder
Scott Hilton

Chief Editor
Colin Edwards

Contributing Editors
Belinda Edwards
Kathy Echeverri
Bobbie Keenum
Greg Keeton

Thank you to the leadership
of Scott Hilton and the team at the
That's My Dad Project.

A MESSAGE
TO THE READER

00

from Colin Edwards
Chief Editor, *That's My Dad Project*

As I sat at my dad's bedside knowing he only had days to live, I had the privilege of pouring my heart out to him. Many don't get this opportunity; I'm incredibly grateful.

I don't know if he could hear me or not as the medicine had him in a sedated state. But, I hope he did.

I thanked him for the hundreds of times he had listened while I navigated through different seasons. I thanked him for the wisdom he poured into my life and for each message he preached that gave me and so many others a fresh perspective on life's circumstances. As I recalled many special memories, I thanked him for the countless hours he had spent coaching me, shooting basketball with me, and throwing ball with me.

Furthermore, I thanked him for the difficult moments when he had to discipline me, even when I was frustrated. I thanked him for the times he didn't give up on me when I went through seasons of rebellion. I thanked him for speaking life over me and regularly reminding me that there was great purpose for my life. I thanked him for giving his life to raising me and my brother, Kyle, and for praying for us fervently, believing that the fullness of that purpose would, one day, be fulfilled in both of us.

Nearly seven years have gone by since my dad passed away. I'm so grateful that Scott gave me the opportunity to be a part of his vision with the That's My Dad Project. After sitting behind the camera and having a front row seat to each of the stories we've documented in this book, I've become even more thankful. Hearing each man tell his

A MESSAGE TO THE READER

story, I wept. In some cases, I was broken hearted about the journey they had been forced to walk. In other instances, I was overwhelmingly inspired by the standard of sacrifice and commitment their dads had set. Through it all, I was reminded how blessed I was to have a dad like I had.

Honestly, it's been one of the greatest joys of my life to put this book together. It's been my highest honor to steward the treasured stories of these men, as I have aimed to tell each one in a way that does it justice.

To the young man who will soon be a father, may these stories birth a fiery passion in you to become the best dad you can be.

To the dad considering walking out on your child, may these stories awaken your heart to the joy and reward that you'll find as you remain committed to them.

To the dad who endured horrific trauma while growing up, may these stories shed light on the freedom that is found in forgiveness and inspire you to break the cycle, making life better for your kids.

To the dad who's been consistent, honorable, and committed through the years, thank you. May these stories spur you on all the more and remind you to finish well.

My prayer is that these stories will mark your life like they've marked mine.

Colin and his wife, Lauren

Colin (right) standing next to his mom, dad, and brother, Kyle

THE MEN WHO SHARED THEIR STORY

Norris Hilton	Anonymous Guest
Mike Wilcut	James Kelley
Taylor Gallman	Todd Walker
David Williams	James Anderson
Ty Harris	Kenneth Bruce
Tommie Goggans	Elijah Clark
Arthur Crumpler	Ric Callahan
Andy Hiti	James Spann
Dan Woodcock	Tyler Hewitt
Alberto Echeverri	Mike Davis
Derek Franklin	Brian Mintz
Zack Franklin	Willie Sayles
Keith Owenbsy	Blake Hamby
Tommy Marshall	Dusty Wright
Walter Smith	Raymond Farmer
Gary Keylon	Jamie Strange
Jerome Thomas	Rene Zeringue
Mark Price	Ty Dillon
Charlie Parker	Kenneth Malone
Brick Haley	Vista McDuffie
James Pullen	Jacob Graul
Cris Mahy	Todd Carnes
Mike McClellan	Eddie Nichols
Dustin Freeman	Jeff Wall
Tony Reddick	Scott Hilton

**To each of you, your vulnerability is shifting a generation.
Thank you.**

INTRODUCTION

"After 50 episodes, the stories are what stand out most."

In January, 2022, we set out to interview 50 fathers to find out what it really takes to be a great dad.

We turned a 12x24 foot shed into a podcast studio, turned on the lights, set up the microphones, and hit record. Then, we sat back and listened to men from drastically different upbringings - from the most horrific to the most beautiful - share about their journey.

We watched as grown men broke down in tears while sharing their story. Some tears were birthed in devastation as their dad had abandoned them. Some tears were filled with joy as they recalled the many special moments they shared with their dad. Some tears came forth from the deep ache that was left after their dad passed away.

After 50 episodes, the stories are what stand out most. That's why our team put this book together - the world needs to hear them.

Some stories feature a specific moment when a dad's action won his daughter's heart, while others shed light on a dad's lifetime of consistency.

Other stories honor the man or woman who stepped into a fatherless child's life, whose sacrifice has shifted the trajectory of that child's family tree.

Whichever the case, one thing is certain: every dad needs to read these stories.

The messages deeply ingrained in this book will break cycles of generational fatherlessness and inspire fathers to become great dads.

CONTENTS

01 **IT ALL STARTED WITH DAD**
Norris Hilton

02 **20 MINUTES I'VE NEVER FORGOTTEN**
Keith Owensby

03 **100 YEARS OF ALCOHOLISM**
Tommy Marshall

04 **DAD TOOK ME TO THE EMERGENCY ROOM**
Kenneth Bruce

05 **I WISH I'D TOLD HIM I LOVED HIM**
Jeff Wall

06 **A FATHER'S HEART & AN EMPTY ORPHANAGE**
Cris Mahy

07 **D-1 QB BREAKS DOWN IN TEARS**
Jamie Strange

08 **SON, I'M PROUD OF YOU**
Daniel Woodcock

09 **A FOOTBALL COACH AND A FATHERLESS BOY**
Dusty Wright & Raymond Farmer

10 **WALKING INTO HEAVEN**
Arthur Crumpler

11 **I BLAMED MYSELF FOR DAD'S DEATH**
Charlie Parker

12 **HAVING TO APOLOGIZE TO MY WIFE AND KIDS**
Tommie Goggans

13 **THE LOST TREASURE**
Andy Hiti

14 **DADDY'S SHOES AND A STRANGER**
Alberto Echeverri

15 **THE DAY DAD SOLD MY JEEP**
Dustin Freeman

16 **THE DAY DAD CAUGHT FIRE**
Anonymous Guest

17 **ATHLETE'S WORLD GETS ROCKED**
Brick Haley

18 **THE DAY DAD BECAME HERO**
Gary Keylon

19 **EPIC CHRISTMAS SURPRISE FOR THE KIDS**
Derek Franklin

20 **SLUSHEES AND GATORADES**
Blake Hamby

21 **THE LETTER DAD KEPT**
Todd Carnes

22 **DON'T GET RID OF THE DINNER TABLE!**
Scott Hilton

23 **WHY THEIR SON WOULDN'T EAT DINNER**
Jamie Strange

24 **DAD/DAUGHTER DATES**
Willie Sayles

25 **A FATHERLESS BOY - A FATHER TO MANY**
Tony Reddick

26 **WHEN A GUY WANTS TO MARRY YOUR DAUGHTER**
Walter Smith

27 **LOOKING FOR DAD IN THE STANDS**
Brian Mintz

28 **I FOUND OUT THE TRUTH... 18 YEARS LATER**
Tyler Hewitt

29 **PASTOR CUTS REVIVAL SERVICE SHORT**
Norris Hilton

30 **DRUGS & A FRYING PAN**
Elijah Clark

31 **A RUDE AWAKENING FOR THIS PASTOR**
Keith Owensby

32 **DAD QUIT HIS DREAM JOB**
Kenneth Bruce

33	**YOU HAVE BABE RUTH'S AUTOGRAPH?!** Ric Callahan	49	**THE GREATEST MEMORY I HAVE WITH DAD** Eddie Nichols
34	**DAD KILLED SEVEN PEOPLE** Vista McDuffie	50	**A STORY OF REDEMPTION** Mike Wilcut
35	**TWO SONS AND A SWORD** Cris Mahy	51	**FORGIVING MOM AND STEPDAD** Dustin Freeman
36	**SLEEPWALKING LOOKING FOR DAD** Jerome Thomas	52	**FIRST TIME HEARING, "SON, I LOVE YOU"** Taylor Gallman
37	**WAR HEROES REUNITED 50 YEARS LATER** Mike Davis	53	**ABUSED. NEGLECTED. I WOULDN'T CHANGE IT.** James Kelley
38	**DAD LIVED DOWN THE STREET ALL THIS TIME** Walter Smith	54	**A FATHER'S BELIEF IN HIS SON** Ty Harris
39	**FIVE GENERATIONS OF GODLY FATHERS** James Pullen	55	**A TRUCK STOP IN TEXAS** James Anderson
40	**I CALLED MY 78-YEAR-OLD DAD** Mark Price	56	**A FATHER TO MANY** Eddie Nichols
41	**THE HAMBY FAMILY PLAN** Blake Hamby	57	**THROWING BALL WITH DAD** Brian Mintz
42	**DAD DIDN'T GIVE UP ON ME** Jacob Graul	58	**A TRADITION LIKE NONE OTHER** Mike Davis
43	**ABANDONED AT AGE 7** James Spann	59	**NEVER CALL ME AGAIN** Anonymous Guest
44	**NO IDEA HOW DAD PULLED THAT OFF** Rene Zeringue	60	**THE POWER OF ADOPTION** Rene Zeringue
45	**A FRUSTRATING HOME LIFE, A RUNAWAY CHILD** Mike McClellan	61	**TURNING DOWN THE OPPORTUNITY OF A LIFETIME** Taylor Gallman
46	**ON THE JOB TRAINING** Kenneth Malone	62	**DAD KISSED MOM!** Todd Walker
47	**DAD WOKE ME UP AT THE FRAT HOUSE** Mark Price	63	**WHEN I FOUND OUT I WAS GONNA BE A DAD** David Williams
48	**EXPOSURE EXPANDS EXPECTATION** Ty Dillon		

DAD STORIES

IT ALL STARTED WITH DAD

Norris and his son, Scott, holding the actual football used that afternoon back in 1977

01

01

IT ALL STARTED WITH DAD

Norris Hilton

It was a Saturday afternoon in 1977. It wasn't just an ordinary Saturday afternoon. It was a Saturday in the fall. In the South, that only means one thing - college football. More specifically, Alabama football. Norris Hilton, an avid Crimson Tide fan, had been counting down the days until Bear Bryant and the Crimson Tide would take on the, then-ranked, #1 USC Trojans. Norris had his Orville Redenbacher popcorn ready to go and leaned back in his recliner as the game was about to kick off.

All of a sudden, Scott, his ten-year-old boy, came running into the living room and obliviously asked his dad to come outside and be the all-time quarterback for his and his friends' game of backyard football. The neighborhood boys, as they often did on Saturdays, had all gathered together and they were short one player. Scott knew just the guy to call.

Without hesitation, Norris hopped out of his recliner, left his freshly-popped popcorn on the side table, and headed outside to play ball with his son just as the Alabama game was underway.

All the kids cheered as their all-time quarterback made his way across the yard and the game began! For those unfamiliar with backyard football, the rule goes like this: The defense has to count five "Mississippi's" before they can rush the quarterback but when they do rush, the quarterback can run. That's exactly what happened. Scott was on defense, counted five "Mississippi's" as fast as he could, darted towards his dad, only to be left with a mouthful of dirt as his dad busted a move on him. Norris left the rest of them in the dust. As he crossed the make-shift goal line, Scott proudly said, "That's my dad! That's my dad!" Scott was embarrassed about being juked by "an old guy," but smiled in pride because his dad had chosen him over the highly-anticipated football game. His dad wasn't going to miss out on time with his son.

DAD STORIES

20 MINUTES I'VE NEVER FORGOTTEN

Keith with his dad, Stanley, in front of the same pond where his dad went fishing with him 45 years ago

02

20 MINUTES I'VE NEVER FORGOTTEN

Keith Owensby

While Keith was growing up, his dad, Stanley, was a traveling evangelist, so he was often away from home. Nevertheless, Keith's dad made sure he knew his son was loved unconditionally and made every effort to spend quality time with him. Even when Stanley would preach a multi-day revival three hours away, he would still make the drive home every night just to be with his family. Then, he'd get up the next morning and make that same three-hour drive to preach the service, and then return home again to be with his family that night. He did this for many, many years.

For several days, Keith, who was a young boy at the time, had been asking his dad to go fishing with him in their pond that was just behind the house in the backyard. It was a beautiful afternoon, and Keith began to get his fishing clothes on and gather the fishing gear. As he rounded the corner with the rods and tackle box, his dad was walking out the door in his suit. He had a three hour drive to make to get to the revival service.

Stanley, seeing his son was ready to go fishing with him, went back into the bedroom, took off his suit, put on his fishing clothes and walked to the pond where he spent twenty minutes fishing with his son. After twenty minutes, he headed back inside, put his suit back on, got in the car, and drove three hours to preach.

Today, Keith is 55 years old. It's been nearly fifty years since those twenty minutes took place, but as Keith puts it, it's "twenty minutes I've never forgotten."

DAD STORIES

100 YEARS OF ALCOHOLISM

03

Tommy with his wife and two grandchildren

03

100 YEARS OF ALCOHOLISM

Tommy Marshall

Tommy's dad was a "full-blown alcoholic," oftentimes drinking for weeks on end. He was known throughout the community as the town drunk and was arrested eleven times in one month for "drinking and tearing the city up." To make matters even worse, the alcoholic cycle led him to be abusive toward Tommy's mom. This violence created a tumultuous life for Tommy and his sisters. On several instances, Tommy and his mom and siblings would have to leave the house and sleep on park benches or in the back of a car because Tommy's dad had quite literally destroyed the home.

If it weren't for Tommy's mom, there's no telling where he and his sisters would have ended up. She would take a beating on Saturday night, then be at church on Sunday morning. She was steadfast, loving, and persevering. Her priority was her children, and they stood together through it all. Tommy still has the utmost appreciation for her to this day.

It's interesting that Tommy's dad, granddad, and great-granddad were all alcoholics. This life-destroying issue was generational and had been passed down for nearly 100 years.

When Tommy was in ninth grade, he was called out of class and instructed to go home to check on his dad. When he arrived home, he found his dad lying in a puddle of vomit. After dragging him to the bathroom and helping him stand up, the two had a conversation.

Tommy asked his dad, "Dad, why are you doing this to us? Why are you destroying our family?" His dad replied, "Son, I'm just trying to escape. When I get drunk, I don't have to think about the things that have been done to me and the things I've done to others."

Tommy began to understand that his dad was abused growing up and had to endure significant trauma in an unstable home. Tommy realized that his dad had fallen prey to the only cycle he had ever known.

Later, as a young adult, Tommy faced a difficult decision. While looking down at a contract that meant a lucrative music career, he had to decide if it was really worth leaving his family to travel the country pursuing fame and success. Ultimately, he had to decide if he was going to be the first to choose his family over anything else and be the one to break the cycle. Tommy stood up in the room where his agent and the executives of the record company sat and said, "I'm going back to Gadsden. This meeting is over." He took a firm stance and made it clear that his first priority was his wife and daughter. They stood up and stopped him, promising that they could get him as many wives as he wanted. Tommy kept walking.

For the first time in nearly a century, a man in the Marshall family line chose his family. Today, Tommy is a committed husband, a loving father, and a proud poppa. He is the pastor at the Tabernacle in Gadsden, Alabama. He has committed his life to helping people escape situations like the one he had to overcome.

Tommy and his family

DAD STORIES

DAD TOOK ME TO THE EMERGENCY ROOM

04

Kenneth and his wife, Kristy, and their five children: Noah, Adoniram, Asa, Nathan, and Ellie Ann.

04

DAD TOOK ME TO THE EMERGENCY ROOM

Kenneth Bruce

As a teenager, Kenneth was in a terrible car accident. The wreck could have killed him because he wasn't wearing a seatbelt. Yet, miraculously, he was not hurt at all.

After it was clear that Kenneth was okay, his dad learned that his son wasn't wearing his seatbelt. He took it upon himself to teach his son a lesson he would never forget.

At the time, Kenneth's dad was the Administrator at the local hospital so he had access to the emergency room. He and Kenneth hopped in the vehicle and drove directly to the local hospital's emergency room and waited. He sat half the night and waited for the perfect moment to teach his son a life-long lesson. Confused, Kenneth wondered what in the world they were doing there. He wasn't aware of it at the time, but his dad was waiting for an accident victim to come into the ER.

Before too long, the tragic moment arrived. A mangled body was rolled into the ER. The individual had been in a vehicle accident and was not wearing a seatbelt. His dad led him into the unit and Kenneth got a good look at what could've been him earlier that day.

This is a brutal, yet beautiful picture of a father who loved his son greatly and wanted him to be protected if an accident were to happen again. This life- shifting moment still resonates with him today.

DAD STORIES

I WISH I'D TOLD HIM I LOVED HIM

Jeff (right), his wife, and their two children

05

I WISH I'D TOLD HIM
I LOVED HIM

Jeff Wall

Jeff Wall was one of eight siblings. Even though his dad struggled as an alcoholic, he loved his children greatly and did his best to provide through his job as a truck driver.

Jeff and his dad were particularly close, and Jeff would often accompany him on his long trips. He recalls wonderful childhood memories of riding alongside his dad on long trips and eating bologna sandwiches together. When Jeff was sixteen years old, his dad suffered a massive heart attack. Miraculously, he survived, but the loss of his income forced the family into public housing. A few months later, Jeff's dad was hospitalized again.

Jeff didn't know it at the time, but the routine visit to check in on Dad while he recovered would be the last time he saw his dad alive. As he walked out, Jeff's dad said, "Love you, son!" Jeff, expecting to see his dad again the following day, didn't say it back.

It would be a moment that he still struggles with immensely to this day because, just a few hours later, his dad passed away.

When the visitation for the family began, it took Jeff three hours to muster up the courage to walk to his dad's casket. But, he did it. It's been over thirty years since his dad passed and Jeff is continuing to find healing from it. He clings tightly to the memories they shared together and lives by the things his dad taught him. He's a faithful husband and a wonderful father to two successful children.

When Jeff was asked what he would tell his dad if he were here today, tears formed in his eyes. He replied, "Love you, too."

DAD STORIES

A FATHER'S HEART AND AN EMPTY ORPHANAGE

Cris and his daughter, Karina

06

A FATHER'S HEART AND
AN EMPTY ORPHANAGE

Cris Mahy

When Cris Mahy was a young man, he asked God to give him "a father's heart." As he prayed this, he had no idea what God would soon do.

When an opportunity arose for Cris to go to Ukraine, he got his paperwork in order and headed to Europe. On the third day of his trip, he traveled to an orphanage with a group of people. Before this trip, Cris and his wife had been resource parents time and time again, which meant that they would house kids from a local boys' home for a weekend once a month. Cris was accustomed to spending time with orphaned kids.

In Ukraine, while he was taking some photos at the orphanage, some music began to play and a host of Ukrainian kids came out and began to dance to the music. During the dance, one young girl kept looking towards Cris, and they locked eyes several times. Something was happening in Cris' heart as he found himself fighting back tears. Right there, while he was taking photos, Cris had an encounter with the Lord.

Cris heard the Lord speak to his spirit, "Take these kids to be yours. I'm calling you to be a father." Unable to hold back the tears at this point, something huge was being birthed in his heart. God was doing exactly what Cris had prayed for. God was giving him a heart for these children. Throughout the rest of the trip, he couldn't shake this moment and began to ponder on what this meant for his life.

By the time Cris arrived home, he had clarity. He went to his wife and said,

"Karen, we've got to adopt." They prayed and sought God's direction and then began the long process of international adoption. A year from when Cris first traveled to Ukraine, they both flew to Ukraine together. After several weeks of being in Ukraine, they traveled to a remote village, which is where they met Karina, the teenage girl who would soon become their daughter.

While sitting before the government officials finalizing paperwork, Cris made a promise to them. He vowed, "Someday, we'll bring Karina back here." The officials scoffed at him because, often, parents would adopt kids into difficult, unstable circumstances and never bring them back. They didn't believe Cris even for a second.

Two years later, they kept their promise and took Karina back to Ukraine. As the Ukrainian officials saw the smile on her face, along with how healthy and happy she looked, they began to cry. They looked at Cris and, to his complete shock, said, "Now, we want to tell you - because of your faithfulness in bringing her back, we will not only open this orphanage to you anytime you want to come… you can bring anyone you want to bring with you to tell these kids about your God." That's how "Mercy's Hope" was born - a ministry that would impact hundreds of kids' lives by loving and caring for each one in Mercy's Hope sponsored "Hope Homes." In addition, they sent teams into Ukraine to minister and love on the kids in this orphanage.

In a story beyond belief, within ten years, the original orphanage where Karina lived closed because there were no more kids. They had all been adopted into Christian homes with great families.

Cris with Scott after his interview on the "That's My Dad Podcast"

DAD STORIES

THE TEARS OF A DIVISION-1 QUARTERBACK

Jamie (right) with his three sons

07

07

THE TEARS OF A DIVISION-1 QUARTERBACK

Jamie Strange

Jamie Strange is one of the Directors of the Fellowship of Christian Athletes in North Alabama. An influential man in the community, he's given much of his life to intentionally investing in the lives of youth and young adults. Sometimes, it's a conversation. Other times, it's just showing up to their games. Regardless, he wants these young kids to know he cares for them and is in their corner.

When Jamie was the Chaplain of the Jacksonville State University Football Team, his responsibility and passion was to build relationships with the players and be a challenging, yet encouraging voice for them as they journeyed through their careers. Many of these players were navigating extremely difficult circumstances. On the field, they looked like star athletes with a bright future... and they absolutely were. But, on the inside, many of them were trying to overcome the hurt and trauma they experienced because their father wasn't the father he needed to be.

There was one particular player who was a stud of an athlete and played a significant role in the team's success. After some behavioral issues and a handful of warnings, the team had to take disciplinary action and let him go. Jamie found out and immediately called him on the phone asking, "Want to get some lunch?" To Jamie's surprise, the young man agreed. This young man had formerly made joking remarks behind Jamie's back like "that ole preacher man" and "Ah, here goes the preacher man again." But, those words didn't phase Jamie. He was just glad they were going to get to talk.

When they sat down to eat, Jamie said, "Man, I'm sorry. I just want you to know I'm here to support you in any way I can." Then, to his surprise, this

DAD STORIES

Division-1 athlete broke down in tears and began to voice the frustration he had carried for many years. "Man, nobody taught me how to treat a woman. Nobody talked to me about what I wanted to do with my life. It's just been football. I don't have any kind of plan."

This 21-year-old had grown up fatherless. He had no example. He didn't have anyone step in and he didn't have a clue how to navigate these issues. Sadly, this young man's story represents the stories of millions of other young men who had no example. Things look alright when we see them experiencing success in sports and in their career. But on the inside, they are navigating some massive issues and are desperate for direction.

Jamie stood in the gap that day and took that young man under his wing.

Jamie with Scott after his interview on the "That's My Dad Podcast"

DAD STORIES

SON, I'M PROUD OF YOU

Dan, his dad, and two sons after running together in the Barbarian Challenge

"SON, I'M PROUD OF YOU"

Daniel Woodcock

Dan and his dad had tension for many years. His dad was a military man who led his home much like he led his subordinates - stern, strict, and hard. In their household, this created difficulty and strain in the relationship he had with his son. When Dan was thirteen-years-old, his dad became a pastor and Dan had a difficult time adjusting to being a preacher's kid. The tension became stronger and he continued to develop even more resentment toward both his dad and the church.

This resentment soon led to rebellion. Dan put on a front for his dad in church; yet, he would live differently around his buddies. They grew even more distant. A mission trip to Mexico would prove to be a turning point in Dan's life as he began to feel a shift in his heart. In a bizarre turn of events, he began to sense that God was calling him into full-time ministry. Don't forget that, prior to this, Dan wanted nothing to do with the church.

The shift in his heart and the urgent desire he was experiencing became too much to resist. Dan began to explore the idea of going to a Bible college in Springfield, Missouri. His dad struggled with the thought of this. Their family's church experience was largely traditional with all men wearing suits and only singing hymns. His dad believed that anything beyond their experience was contrary to his son's best interest. Dan, against his father's wishes, decided to move to Springfield, which only strengthened the tension between them.

Several years into his ministry, Dan's ministry was making an impact wherever he went. He had just finished speaking at a conference in Boise, Idaho, which wasn't far from where his parents lived. Sitting at lunch with his mom and dad before heading to the airport, his dad looked across the table at his son. In a moment Dan has never forgotten, his dad said, "Son, I'm proud of you." After hearing those words, Dan found himself emotional and was caught completely off guard by how it made him feel. He didn't realize how he had longed to hear those words from his father's mouth.

Dan and his dad now talk often and have a great relationship. He is a committed husband and father of three. He is the senior pastor of Cornerstone Church in Gadsden, Alabama, where he leads hundreds of people from all walks of life on a weekly basis. He goes overboard telling his kids how proud he is and makes sure to let them know each day.

Dan, his wife, and their three children

DAD STORIES

A FOOTBALL COACH AND A FATHERLESS BOY

Dusty and Coach Farmer

Dusty as manager of Etowah's football team

A FOOTBALL COACH AND
A FATHERLESS BOY

Coach Raymond Farmer & Dusty Wright

Dusty was born with cerebral palsy due to a medical accident at birth. His birth father, seeing the struggle that was going to come, abandoned him. His mom stayed committed to him and raised Dusty as a single parent. She worked hard to provide for herself and Dusty, sacrificing to be sure her son was taken care of.

Schools tried to place Dusty in a contained classroom, but his mother fought to have him placed in a regular class. After much debate, the school system honored Dusty's mother's wishes and Dusty was placed in a regular classroom with an aide - a man who would become the first of many father figures to him. After two years with the aide, Dusty requested the opportunity to do it on his own. Seeing his progress and determination, they agreed. In middle school, a football coach approached Dusty and asked him if he wanted to be the statistician for the football team.

Having no idea how much it would change the trajectory of his life, Dusty jumped at the opportunity and quickly developed a love for the game of football and for being a part of the team. As he transitioned into high school, he called the high school coach, Raymond Farmer, and asked if he was in need of a team manager. Coach Farmer agreed to take him but warned him up front: "Just know that you'll be treated like everyone else on the team."

Coach Farmer didn't hold back. If Dusty did something wrong, he got chewed out for it. If he did something well, he was celebrated. For the first time, Dusty wasn't viewed as one with a disability.

Dusty became a central piece of the team. He gave some pre-game speeches to get the guys fired up, while the players continued to rally around him. Dusty was just as much a part of the team as the players were - and there were some good ones. During Dusty's junior year, the team had an undefeated season and won the 5A state championship.

Sadly, after several seasons, it was time for Dusty to graduate, which meant the several years he had so greatly enjoyed were coming to an end. Dusty's progress, confidence, work ethic, and belief in himself had grown immeasurably under the wing of Coach Raymond Farmer.

The story could've ended at graduation and it still would be a great story of how a young boy with physical challenges became an integral part of a special season. It would tell the story of how a legendary, championship-winning football coach took a fatherless kid with cerebral palsy under his wing and made a difference in his life. But, it doesn't end there, not by a long shot.
Over 20 years have gone by since that state championship season. For every one of those years, Coach Farmer and Dusty have gone to lunch together almost every Friday. Coach Farmer continues to intentionally be a father to him. When his mom was in the hospital, Coach would go over to his house and shave his face several times a week.

Because Coach Farmer and several other men stepped into Dusty's path along the way, Dusty Wright is where he is today. Although he still deals with the physical challenges of his condition, he has never expected anything to be handed to him. He gets out of bed, works hard, ensures that his mom is well taken care of, and is now a real estate investor. He is a constant encourager and lifts up the people that are around him. His story has made an impact on thousands of people.

Dusty recently retired after working for twenty-one years with the city of Gadsden. His story shows the world what's possible when a man steps into the life of a fatherless boy.

Dusty and Coach Farmer

Dusty and his mom

Dusty and Coach Farmer with Scott Hilton after their interview on the That's My Dad Podcast

DAD STORIES

I THOUGHT I HAD WALKED INTO HEAVEN

Arthur Crumpler as a young boy

I THOUGHT I HAD WALKED INTO HEAVEN

Arthur Crumpler

The Arthur Crumpler story should be made into a movie. There's no doubt about it. It is the story of a young boy who was raised in poverty and never knew his dad, but defied the statistical odds and, today, has found a way to become a great dad to his daughter.

Although he never knew his dad, Arthur was raised by a hard-working single mother in an economically-deprived, but loving home. One day, as an 18-year-old, he was quite literally walking down the street kicking a can when a neighbor drove up and asked if he wanted to ride to the local community college with him. It is important to note that Arthur had never been there. He knew nothing but his own home and run-down community. When Arthur arrived at Gadsden State, he thought he'd arrived in Heaven. There were nice buildings, air conditioning, and luxuries he had never experienced.

Education was not even an afterthought. It was too expensive. To say it was "out of the realm of possibility" was an understatement for the ages. There was no chance Arthur's mom could afford it. He followed his neighbor into the financial aid office and, suddenly, a conversation arose about Arthur's future and how Gadsden State could play a role in it. Although, deep down, it was a dream to attend college, he quickly dismissed it, believing it wasn't even logical to talk about it.

The financial aid worker shared that Arthur might be eligible for a Pell Grant. Arthur didn't know what a Pell Grant was but, being well-acquainted with the specifics of their income and financial situation, he completed the application anyway. Arthur never dreamed that the Pell Grant would be granted and mark a turning point in his family tree for generations to come. When Arthur found out it was approved, he was "over the moon," but was quickly deflated when he was informed that his first tuition payment was due the next day - to the tune of "a whopping $450." As Arthur put it, "Believe me, that was a lot of money." Because the Pell Grant would not be initiated for several days, they had to come up with the payment up front.

When Arthur wearily approached his mom and let her know about the situation, she stunned him. Without hesitation, the next morning, she and Arthur went to the bank and borrowed $450. Arthur took the money and went straight to Gadsden State to make the payment. He was officially enrolled as a college student. His mom's decision would launch Arthur into a future beyond his wildest dreams.

The Pell Grant was enough to afford Arthur the opportunity to live on campus where there was A/C and enough for him to have three meals a day. Arthur said, "I thought I'd died and gone to Heaven."

Fast forward 55 years... Arthur now holds five advanced college degrees and is a retired school administrator. More importantly, he's fulfilling his lifelong dream of being a great father. Many would wonder: How did this man who never met his dad become a great dad, himself?

For years, even as a growing teenager, Arthur kept his eyes peeled and watched. He would select certain men that stood out to him and observe the way they lived. He watched as one man kept his car washed, another kept his yard in good order, another spent a great deal of time at home, another paid bills on time, and another stayed out of jail. He took the good traits of each man and applied them to his own life, making it his goal to embody each of them.

His daughter's admiration, honor, and respect are evidence that he did it and did it well. Arthur flipped the script!

Arthur's High School Portrait

Arthur with his daughter

DAD STORIES

I BLAMED MYSELF FOR DAD'S DEATH

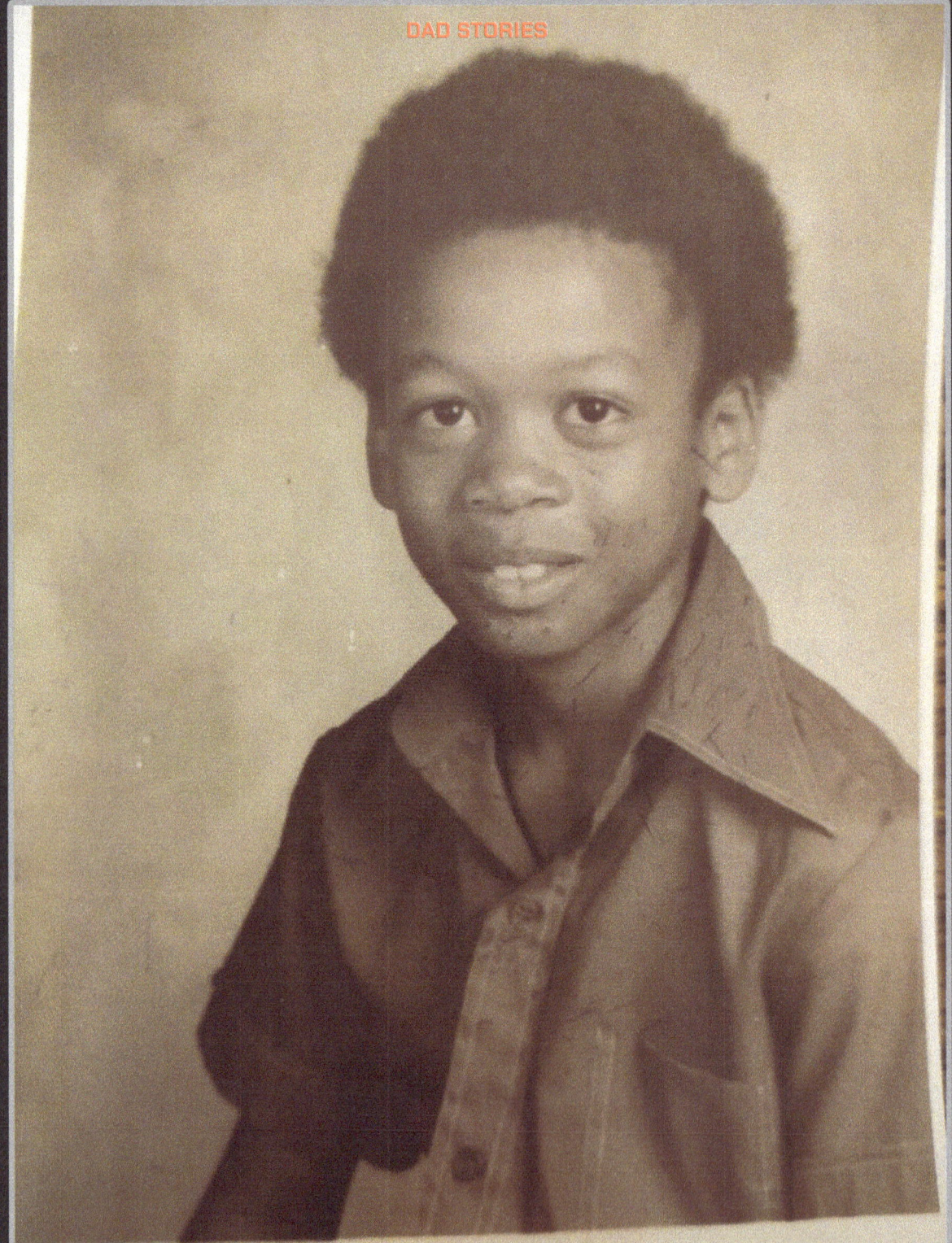

Charlie as a young boy

I BLAMED MYSELF FOR DAD'S DEATH

Charlie Parker

Charlie was one of nine children born to his mother. In the episode, Charlie talks about the many challenges of growing up with eleven people living in a three-bedroom house. Charlie's dad wasn't home much, so it was just his mom and siblings most of the time.

His biological dad passed away when he was only five years old. His mom remarried, and the man she married became a stepdad to her nine children. This man is the one who raised Charlie but, tragically, when Charlie was twelve, his stepdad passed away.

His passing caused Charlie overwhelming grief and pain. Before becoming a teenager, he had lost two dads. No one knew it at the time, but Charlie blamed himself for his stepdad's death. He kept a secret for over twenty years about something that happened just a few hours before his stepdad passed.

Earlier that day, Charlie was at the store with some buddies who lured him into stealing caps for their cap guns. Charlie tried to resist the pressure from his peers but gave in to the pressure and stuffed the caps in his jacket and walked out of the store towards his house. Overcome with guilt and fearful of the potential consequences, he frantically and repeatedly told the guys, "Something bad is going to happen, something bad is going to happen."

The day went on. He and his friends were outside shooting their cap guns at Charlie's house just a few days before Christmas. Later that night, there was a commotion on the other side of the home. Charlie and his siblings hurried across the house and he saw his stepdad laying on the floor. He was unresponsive. They later found out he had died from a heart attack. Standing over his stepdad and trying to come to grips with what was happening before his eyes, Charlie ran outside and over to a neighbor's house. In a panic, he was telling himself, "It's my fault, it's my fault." As his stepdad's body was rolled out of the house that night, Charlie tucked the secret away.

Years went by and Charlie still held this sense of blame. "If I had not stolen the caps, Dad would still be alive." One can imagine how traumatizing this would be for such a young boy.

Charlie carried the pain with him without telling a soul for over two decades. It had nearly destroyed him. As a grown man, he finally got the courage to tell someone about that dreaded day from his childhood. Once he did, he began to experience freedom and healing from the false guilt he had carried for the majority of his life, setting him free to be the husband and father he longed to be. Charlie surrendered his life to Jesus Christ and, after healing from the trauma of those events, is now able to share his story with many young men.

Charlie and his mom

Charlie and his family

DAD STORIES

HAVING TO APOLOGIZE TO MY WIFE AND KIDS

Tommie's family

HAVING TO APOLOGIZE TO MY WIFE AND KIDS

Tommie Goggans

Tommie Goggans will be the first to tell you about the mistake he made one Saturday. It was the Alabama-Auburn football game in 2013. If you're from the South or a college football fan in general, you don't have to be told the details of this November afternoon. It's a story that's since been dubbed, "The Kick Six."

Auburn's Chris Davis caught Alabama's game-winning field goal attempt and took it 109 yards for a touchdown to win the highly-anticipated Iron Bowl as time expired. Well, Tommie and his family are huge Alabama fans. As the madness ensued and Auburn's student body and fan base stormed onto the field in triumph at Jordan-Hare Stadium, Tommie was frantically trying to wrap his head around what had just taken place. His wife spoke up and, as many other fans were doing in hindsight, began to question Alabama's decision to attempt such a long kick.

Tommie, seated in disbelief in the living room with his eight kids and his wife, snapped harshly towards his wife, "kindly" reminded her that her comment was bogus, and then went on a fierce rant in frustration.

Tensions settled. Tommie began to come to grips with the fact that Auburn had just beaten Alabama in one of the craziest fashions in the history of college football. Then, conviction began to settle in as he knew he had let the emotions of the moment cause him to speak disrespectfully towards his wife. To make matters worse, he had done it in front of his kids.

Later that night, he gathered his kids and wife and sat them down. In both embarrassment and humility, he began to express his sincere apologies and reminded his kids that a football game should never have caused him to react that way - even if it is something he's passionate about. Furthermore, he told his kids that he should not have talked to their Mom that way and apologized to her in front of them. Tommie's humble response to his own mistake sets the standard for all dads!

Tommie and his wife

DAD STORIES

THE LOST TREASURE

Andy and his family after a water balloon fight

THE LOST TREASURE

Andy Hiti

Those who know Andy Hiti know him as a soft-spoken, gentle giant (he's 6'4") who runs into burning houses by day as a firefighter and has playful water balloon battles with his sons and grandsons when he gets home. No one would have ever guessed the difficult childhood Andy had to overcome.

Although Andy's dad was always present and worked hard to provide for his family, he was harsh with Andy and his brothers. This was not just some rash words here and there; it was a consistent harshness that Andy had to deal with. Andy, who now is in his 50s, had not heard his dad say, "I love you, son" since he was five years old.

On many occasions, Andy and his dad would play basketball in the backyard, and his dad would play physical ball in an effort to "toughen him up." That physicality often led to cheap shots and sometimes blood from a hit nose or busted lip.

This may sound odd, but the harsh words spoken were more painful than the physical play on the court. This perceived tension was present throughout Andy's childhood and teenage years causing strain on his relationship with his dad.

One day, as an eight-year-old boy, Andy locked himself in the bathroom just to be alone for a few minutes and, upon staring out the window at the sky and reflecting on his situation, made a vow that he would, one day, love his kids and lead his family the right way. He promised to be a better dad to his kids.

Today, some 50 years later, Andy continues to uphold that vow. He is a committed, loving father to his three sons and is faithful to his wife, Belinda. Together, Andy, Belinda, and their family have given much of their lives to raising young men who come from difficult homes - homes where, in many cases, the father was abusive or absent.

Andy's story came full-circle years later after a violent storm came through and trees crushed much of their home. As the cleanup began, Andy went to recover some older items they had stored away and had not seen years. During this process, Andy found a wedding card that his dad had written in 28 years earlier that he had not remembered receiving. In it, his dad wrote, "I'm proud of you and I love you." It was at this moment that Andy began to see that his dad really did care for him. He really did love him. He just didn't know how to show it. His dad has since passed, but he does not carry resentment or bitterness anymore. He has fully forgiven his dad and has a new perspective on the journey he walked.

Andy and Scott after Andy's interview on the "That's My Dad Podcast"

DAD STORIES

DADDY'S SHOES AND A STRANGER IN SOUTH AMERICA

Alberto, his wife, and their two daughters

14

DADDY'S SHOES AND A STRANGER
IN SOUTH AMERICA

Alberto Echeverri

Before Alberto Echeverri was a renown surgeon in North Alabama, he was growing up in Bogota, Colombia. Many years after Alberto left Bogota to pursue his surgical training in the United States, he, his wife, and two daughters traveled back to the place Alberto once called home.

One afternoon, while they were driving through Bogota enjoying time together, Alberto spotted a family walking by and the dad was not wearing any shoes. Alberto stopped the vehicle at the light, immediately took his shoes off, rolled his window down, and extended the shoes toward the man. With gratitude, the man took the shoes.

Although Alberto's daughters were not surprised by their dad's act of generosity, they were impressed. This one moment is just a glimpse into a home where a father consistently exhibits radical generosity and teaches his kids the importance of serving others. Through all of their endeavors, they'll always remember the standard their father set that afternoon in Bogota.

Dustin and his dad on Dustin's wedding day

THE DAY DAD SOLD MY JEEP

Dustin Freeman

Talk about a lesson learned!

When Dustin graduated, his dad took him to the dealership and co-signed for him to get a jeep - something Dustin had been greatly looking forward to. His dad only had one requirement: "If you miss a payment, I'll put it in the front yard and I'll sell it." Dustin, eager to get his jeep, quickly agreed to his dad's condition.

As time went on, Dustin was managing the payments well until, suddenly, he lost his job and wasn't able to make the money for his payment. He kept quiet about it. He didn't have much money in the bank and didn't have any income. It wasn't long before that payment came due and Dustin couldn't pay it.

A couple of weeks later, his dad received a phone call from the loan company. As soon as the phone call ended, his dad walked straight into his room and, without having a conversation, grabbed the keys to the jeep. He walked outside, pulled all of Dustin's belongings out of the jeep, drove the jeep into the front yard by the road, and placed a for sale sign in it. He sold it that day.

Dustin's dad kept his word and taught his son a lesson he'll never forget.

DAD STORIES

THE DAY DAD CAUGHT FIRE

> Due to the nature of Barry's upbringing, we've changed his name and have not included any photos of him.
>
> The story about his journey growing up is Chapter 59 of this book.

THE DAY DAD CAUGHT FIRE

Anonymous Guest

In a horrific accident, Barry nearly burned to death.

He had worked for a couple days clearing a piece of land for a client and had several trees and some brush piled up ready to burn. Due to a recent rain, he could not seem to get the fire burning. As he had done many times before, he poured some gasoline on the brush, stood back, tossed a match, and hoped for the best. But, the wood still would not burn.

As he was standing there pondering what to do, his phone rang. It was around 1pm. With a bottle of gas in one hand, he reached for the phone with his other when an sudden explosion violently launched Barry into the air. He landed flat on his back.

Barry laid there in excruciating pain, not knowing the damage that had been done. He was able to get off the ground, slowly walk across the yard, and stumble into the house, where his wife saw the severe burns. Although the burns were intense, Barry refused to go to the hospital. His wife applied bandages and he sat still for a little while, suffering through the pain.

When his daughter got home from school to get ready to quickly head to her gymnastics meet, she found her dad sitting in the chair, wrapped in bandages, and in horrific pain. After learning the events of the day, she was just thankful to have her dad.

Barry assured his wife and daughter he would be okay. Then, his daughter began to load the car for the hour-long drive to that evening's meet. As they were about to head out, she looked to the front door and her dad was cautiously making his way towards the car.

That evening, he rode two hours and sat through his daughter's two-hour gymnastics meet. He had made a promise to his daughter that he'd never miss one. He never did. He sat there through the immense pain and cheered for his daughter as she performed.

When they got home later that night, Barry still did not want to go to the hospital. They called a doctor friend that was a doctor, who came over and removed the bandages and cleaned the wounds. For the first time, his daughter saw the gravity of the situation. His beard was completely singed on half of his face. The skin on the back of his legs was burned off, leaving the muscles partially exposed. He had third degree burns on his hands, legs, and face.

His daughter says, "That's the day I knew he would be there for me - no matter what."

You can hear Barry's full story
on YouTube.

Episode 25 of the
"That's My Dad Podcast."

Episode Title: "Never Call Me Again"

DAD STORIES

ATHLETE'S WORLD GETS ROCKED

Brick standing next to his wife and two sons

17

ATHLETE'S WORLD
GETS ROCKED

Brick Haley

Andre "Brick" Haley got his nickname when, as a high schooler, he ran into a brick wall and chipped a brick loose. Brick was a linebacker in high school and earned multiple college scholarship opportunities before signing with Alabama A&M. He received Alabama A&M's Inspiration Award in 1987, was named football MVP in their 1988 season and today, he's in their Hall of Fame. Since college, Brick has been a successful college and NFL coach with a career spanning over 30 years.

To see Brick's success, one would never guess that he grew up in public housing projects in a small home with nine other children. He was the youngest. Although they didn't have much, their home was filled with love. Being raised in this way presented some difficulties for a family so large. Perhaps having to face adversity at such a young age was preparing Brick for the adversity he would face as an adult.

Today, Brick is the proud father of 3 children, whom he loves deeply. His life changed when his son, AJ, was born. As a star athlete himself, Brick had dreams of spending time with his son on the football field together. When this dream was unable to be fulfilled in the way he had envisioned it, it was tough. AJ was on the autism spectrum. Brick spent many years having to fight the disappointment that would try and settle in his heart.

He was never disappointed in his son; he loved AJ deeply but, the dream he had his eyes on would not be fulfilled the way he hoped it would. As time went on, Brick began to discover something powerful - something he would not have discovered if things would have taken place the way he had envisioned.

Brick had this to say about his son:
"AJ is what the world should be about - loving and caring. No matter what my day is like - if we win, lose, whatever, when he hears the garage door come up, he's gonna come and give me a hug when I walk in the door. For me, that's what's important."

In a society and world that places such massive emphasis on wins and losses, Brick calls for each of us to see from a different perspective.

Brick and his family use their platform to raise awareness surrounding autism through "Brick Road to Success." Together, they're helping other families navigate these challenging circumstances. Their story is a reminder to us all of what is really important in life. Brick has three sons: Adrian, A.J. and Jeremy.

Brick has coached in the NFL as well as several Division-1 Universities

DAD STORIES

THE DAY DAD BECAME HERO

Gary and his dad

THE DAY DAD BECAME HERO

Gary Keylon

Gary Keylon's dad was a hard worker. They didn't have much money growing up, but they had a home full of love and Christian values.

When Gary began to develop a passion for sports, his dad took the time to build a weight bench with weights, so he could work out and build the strength he needed to be successful in athletics. This weight set quickly became the centerpiece of their time together and the place of bonding in their relationship. Together, as father and son, they'd do their workouts. They would measure their progress, chart their numbers, and work together to improve their strength. It was a place Gary treasured.

One day, while at school a couple of miles away from home, Gary saw a cloud of dark smoke billowing off in the distance in the direction of his house. He didn't know it at the time, but his dad was fighting an all-out blaze that had started from an oil furnace in their basement. They lived out in middle-of-nowhere Tennessee which meant that it would take firefighters a good deal of time to get their trucks out there. The fire was quickly getting out of hand, shifting his dad's focus from putting it out to saving what he could. His dad had the opportunity to run into the house and grab one thing. Most would have grabbed photo albums, money, or documents. His dad didn't grab those.

When Gary arrived home later that afternoon, he saw the place where his house previously stood. While trying to process what had happened, he looked to his left and there sat his weight set in the front yard. While telling this part of his story, Gary broke down in tears. His dad recognized the value of the weight bench. It wasn't the monetary value that made it worth saving. It was because it had become the place where he and his son had built their relationship together.

The story would come full circle over a decade later as Gary's strength journey that began in that basement with his dad would land him a place on one of the most elite, well-known strength groups to ever travel the world: the Power Team. This ministry would travel the globe doing feats of strength in front of thousands of people on a weekly basis.

It became Gary's platform to share the gospel of Jesus Christ with millions of people.

Gary and his family

Gary and the same weight bench his dad saved in the fire 40 years ago

Gary preaching the Gospel as a member of the Power Team

AN EPIC SURPRISE ON CHRISTMAS DAY

Derek and his family

AN EPIC SURPRISE ON CHRISTMAS DAY

Derek Franklin

Christmas was just around the corner. Derek Franklin and his wife headed to Walmart to stock up on toys for their three kids and they wanted to go "all out." With several shopping carts full of toys their kids had been wanting, they headed toward the bicycle aisle to pick up their final gift. As they looked through the many options, they began to look for a worker to help them with the selection, but all the workers were busy. While they sat there unsure of which route to go, they looked at the carts full of toys and had a moment of questioning. Something felt off.

They were about to spend a lot of money, but would the kids really use these? Would they be beneficial? Is there a better idea? Right there on the spot, they decided to go a different route and do something more meaningful. They wanted to create a space for their kids to hang out.

So, they unloaded each of the shopping carts, placed all the toys back on the shelves, and left Walmart empty-handed with a new plan.

When they arrived home, the plan gained clarity. They were going to completely renovate the building in the backyard that had always been a workshop and turn it into an epic place for the kids to hang out. Hilariously, they let the kids in on the fact that they were going to clean up the workshop and replace some things, but didn't tell them what it was going to become. So, over the next couple of weeks, the kids were in the shop with them renovating the space.

When Christmas morning arrived, the kids were excited! But, they had no idea what was in store. When it came time to open gifts, they opened a few boxes of clothes and were led to believe that it was all they were able to get this year. Being the respectful kids they were, they still showed a great deal of gratitude and appreciation for the clothes they had been given and thanked their parents for a great Christmas.

It was time to unveil the big surprise.

Derek brought a big box into the living room and said, "Alright, here's your big gift!" The kids quickly broke through the big cardboard box only to discover a slightly smaller box inside. In classic parent fashion, Derek and his wife had wrapped box after box after box to heighten the suspense of the big reveal.

After several minutes of tearing through boxes, the kids arrived at the final box - a small, gift-card-sized box taped shut. As they opened it, they found three keys. But Derek and his wife wouldn't tell their three kids which door the keys opened. After thinking it through, the kids hurried out to the workshop and the keys were a perfect fit. They opened the door and walked into a brand new space fitted with games, a sound system, a stage, a disco ball, a snack bar, and everything a kid could dream of.

For all their years in middle and high school, this old workshop became the place where all their friends came to hang out and where they spent a great deal of time together as a family.

Derek and his wife are glad they left the shopping carts behind and exchanged them for something more meaningful - a place where they could create memories as a family.

Derek standing between his dad and his son

SLUSHEES AND GATORADES

Blake and his dad

SLUSHEES AND GATORADES

Blake Hamby

Blake Hamby came from a great family and, still today, has a close relationship with his father. His parents just celebrated their 50-year wedding anniversary.

Blake was asked, "What memories with your dad stand out most to you?"

To many, his answer will seem insignificant. Blake was hesitant to even share it because it wouldn't seem like a big deal. But, he shared it anyways because it meant a lot to him.

The memories that stood out most to him were the many trips he and his dad took to the gas station after football practice. On their way home, they would stop and get a slushy and a Gatorade.

Yep, that's it. That's the memory. That's the one that stood out.

Even today, over 30 years later, each time Blake passes by that gas station, he's reminded of those many times he and his dad would go in together and get a slushy and a Gatorade. It may sound insignificant, but it's been three decades and he still cherishes the memory and tells the story.

This is a message to every father out there. It's the small things that make the biggest difference. It's those small moments that your kid will remember.

DAD STORIES

Todd (right) standing next to his dad and brother

THE LETTER DAD KEPT

Todd Carnes

Todd Carnes' life has been successful in many ways. He has been a missionary in Russia, founded and pastored a healthy, thriving church, spent time in the political space, and authored a book.

To know Todd, one would have no idea how difficult his childhood was. In fact, even his childhood friends who spent much of their time playing backyard football with him, are shocked to hear the stories to this day.

Todd grew up in a home where alcoholism reaped devastating effects. His dad did a lot of great things but was given heavily to alcohol. The drinking would continue for days, even weeks on end, and would turn to cursing, anger, and violence. After 10-14 days, his dad would begin to sober up and return to his normal self, catch up on two weeks of work in his business, stay clean for a couple of months, then fall into the cycle again.

One night, Todd was laying in bed as a young boy while the cursing and violence across the home was ultra-intense. Staring into the darkness, he made a vow that, when he was older, he would never live this way. After many years of this, his dad's body couldn't handle that level of alcohol anymore. The drinking slowed down and so did the violence but, then, a series of affairs then took place. Although Todd was hopeful, the stability of the home never existed. One evening, Todd's father laid his two sons on the bed, leaned over them, and told them it was just not going to work out with their mother so he was leaving. As Todd puts it, "You never forget that."

Despite the vow that Todd made as a young boy, he found himself drifting into the same alcoholic cycle when he was fifteen years old. His good friend, Goose, watched as Todd's life began to spiral much like that of his dad. By the time he was in college, it had become so extreme that those closest to Goose were urging him to stay away from Todd, but he refused.

After his own battle with addiction, Todd was disgusted with himself and knew there had to be more to life than this. One morning, after three days of drinking, he was trying to figure out how to stop the chaos that was now in his own life. Goose came in the door and, in an attempt to throw him a lifeline, "strong-armed" him into going to a Bible Study. Todd, to appease the friend who had stayed by his side, agreed to go. After hearing the beauty of the Gospel, Todd gave his life to Jesus later that night and hasn't been bound by alcohol since. The cycle was miraculously broken after many generations.

In reflection on the traumatic years that were Todd's childhood, he wrote several letters to his dad. In his 20s, he wrote letters expressing the anger and hurt that he had towards his dad for the many years of addiction, affairs, and abuse and even blamed him for his own struggles with alcohol and depression. But in his 40s, as his heart began to shift towards grace and forgiveness, he wrote another letter. He chose to remind his dad of the good things he remembered from his childhood. He chose to thank him for the opportunity to go to school and for taking him fishing. He chose to thank his dad for working hard and single-handedly pulling his family out of poverty. In forgiveness, he thanked him for trying his best.

After his dad died, Todd was looking through all of his belongings in his childhood home where all of the pain and chaos had taken place. It was there that he found this last letter that his father had kept. He was so relieved that he had not only forgiven him, but had expressed it fully.

Todd (left) next to his dad and brother

DAD STORIES

DON'T GET RID OF THE DINNER TABLE!

the dinner table Scott fought to keep still sits in their home today

Scott and his family around the dining room table

DON'T GET RID OF THE DINNER TABLE!

Scott Hilton

Scott and his wife, Diana, were making the time-consuming, often-dreaded preparations of moving homes. Amidst all the boxing up of personal items, taping drawers shut of larger furniture pieces, and thrift store trips with the things they no longer needed, Scott had only one plea: don't get rid of the dinner table.

The dinner table was old. It was beaten up with dings and scratches. With the eye, one would suggest including it in the trip to the thrift store.

Beneath the scratches and dings were years of cherished moments and conversations that would prove to shape the lives of their children and the bond of their family. The dinner table was more than a piece of wood. It was a symbol that represented the growth of their family together. It represented the hundreds of conversations that took place around a home-cooked meal as they addressed each day's issues, shared stories, and created an inseparable bond together.

Today, although the kids are grown and living on their own, that dinner table remains a symbol of family. Scott believes the conversations around that cherished table are a large reason his kids are living productive lives today.

DAD STORIES

WHY OUR 4-YEAR OLD BOY WOULDN'T EAT DINNER

Jamie and his family

WHY OUR 4-YEAR-OLD BOY WOULDN'T EAT DINNER

Jamie Strange

Jamie Strange will be the first to tell you that he's made mistakes. Like any dad, there are things he wishes he would have done better when raising his children.

Before Jamie transitioned to becoming one of the Directors of the Fellowship of Christian Athletes, he had been in full-time ministry at different churches over a span of twenty-seven years. During that season, Jamie would eat dinner with his family, then head out for a few hours on many nights to fulfill some of his ministry responsibilities with other kids' games and pastoral care.

One night, as his family would do often, they were seated around the table for dinner. After serving the meal, he and his wife noticed their four-year-old son wouldn't eat. They sat there for a few minutes wondering why then asked him, "Son, why aren't you eating?" His son replied, "Because when I finish eating, Dad leaves."

This was a reality-check type of moment for Jamie. His four-year-old's statement caught him completely off guard but ended up shifting everything for him as a dad. As any Pastor, church leader, or anyone active in ministry knows, some seasons are overwhelmingly busy. But ever since that moment sitting around the dinner table, Jamie's focus has shifted.

He still gives much of his life to investing in young men, but now makes absolutely sure that his family is his first priority and that his children know they are loved unconditionally.

DAD STORIES

FATHER/DAUGHTER DATES

Willie and his family

FATHER/DAUGHTER
DATES

Willie Sayles

Willie grew up in a house with a hard-working father and a loving mother. From watching his father's example, Willie learned the importance of working hard to provide for his family. Growing up, Willie and his siblings felt "slighted" because their dad had fully given himself to pastoring a church. "He spent more time at the church and more time with the church kids." Willie even recalls that his dad nearly prioritized one of the church's revival services over attending his own son's graduation.

Willie knew he was loved and cared for, but his parents just didn't voice it. One afternoon, Willie overheard his dad say to his buddy from across the room, "You know, I'm really proud of that boy." On another occasion, he heard his mom say to her friend, "I'm really proud of Willie." Even though they never told him directly, he knew they were proud of him. Those are both moments Willie hangs on to.

Today, as a father himself, Willie has made it a point to learn from his experiences as a child and teenager. As a dad of three girls, he goes overboard in voicing how much he loves them. He prioritizes his family over his ministry. Furthermore, he even takes his daughters on daddy/daughter dates on a regular basis. Girl dads, this is something you need to add to your monthly routines!

Willie will let his daughter pick what she wants to do. Then, they'll block off an entire evening and do it together. Sometimes, it's as simple as ordering pizza and watching a couple of movies. Other times, it's dinner at a nicer restaurant and a trip to the mall. Regardless, they're spending quality time together and building memories that will last a lifetime.

DAD STORIES

FATHERLESS BOY BECOMES A FATHER TO MANY

Tony and his son

FATHERLESS BOY BECOMES A
FATHER TO MANY

Tony Reddick

To see Tony Reddick's success today, one would never guess the adversity he faced as a child.

Tony only saw his dad twice. The first time, he was eighteen months old and the second time, he was seventeen years old. His dad simply walked away. As Tony puts it, he was a "wayward guy."

Tony was raised in public housing with a single mother and 8 siblings. The extent of his relationship with his dad was a "Happy Birthday" each year on the phone and a "Happy Father's Day" in June. His dad passed away in 2015.

From a young age, Tony had the determination to show what could be possible in life when one is raised without a father. But, it wasn't only fatherlessness that he had to battle. At the age of four, he was in a car accident and lost sight in his right eye, but his determination wasn't phased. He was still fully committed to learning how to become an honorable man who could persevere through adversity. Even as a young boy, he always recognized men who were doing things the right way. Whether it was a neighbor, a co-worker, a teacher, or a coach, Tony was creating the model dad in his mind by combining the great traits of all these men. Tony even jokes that Fred Flintstone was the Father of the Year.

When Tony was in the seventh grade, he was given the opportunity of a lifetime. His work ethic and success as a student earned him a scholarship to a prestigious private school in Massachusetts. After saying yes to this opportunity, he realized that he had to walk a mile, catch three buses, hop on a train, and walk another mile just to get to school five days a week. It took him two hours each way. By this time, Tony was more acquainted with what it means to persevere through adversity than most grown men so this was not an issue. After several years of hard work, he graduated with honors from this prestigious school and went to college where he, comically, earned a basketball scholarship and never even told the coach that he was blind in one eye.

Today, Tony is the Superintendent of Schools for the Gadsden City Schools system in Gadsden, Alabama where he oversees more than 600 employees and over 5,000 students.

In his free time, he prioritizes heading down to the children's center to mentor students on a one-on-one basis. When asked why he does it, he referenced the men who had stepped into his life and invested in him. Very simply, he said, "I vowed, even as a child, that I would pay that forward for the rest of my life."
An accomplished writer, artist, husband, father, and administrator, it is Tony's greatest joy to now take care of his mother. Tony's life is a story beyond belief. Many recognize his success but aren't aware of what he had to walk through to get there. His story is a beacon that sheds light on what's possible with determination and perseverance.

Tony and his son

DAD STORIES

WHEN A YOUNG MAN WANTS TO MARRY YOUR DAUGHTER

Walter, his daughter, and his wife, Cynthia

WHEN A YOUNG MAN WANTS TO MARRY YOUR DAUGHTER

Walter Smith

It all started at the laundromat on Tuscaloosa Avenue back in the 1970s. Every Saturday, Walter's family made the trip down the street to wash and dry their clothes. One Saturday, there was a moment that sparked the beginning of something special. Walter was eight years old, and as they walked into the laundromat, a young girl caught his eye and stopped him in his tracks. After a few moments of being awestruck, he whispered to his mom, "Mom, I might just marry that girl one day." His mom comically interjected, "Son, you don't know what you're talking about. Get in the car."

Life went on. Walter found out that the beautiful girl lived only a few blocks away, but for the next few years, he tucked the thought away… until middle school.

While in school one morning, Walter crossed paths with the same girl from the laundromat. Cynthia Etheridge was her name and, after some conversation and a little time together, sparks began flying like it was the Fourth of July. They dated all through high school, college, and have now been married for over thirty years. Eight-year-old Walter was right! They still get a kick out of the laundromat story today.

This is more than just a good love story.

Walter was raised without a father, leaving him to figure out much of manhood and fatherhood on his own. When he found Cynthia, he gained more than a wife. Cynthia's father, Mr. Etheridge, was a well-respected, hard-working, successful, family man who led his wife and their ten children well. Knowing Walter's story, Mr. Etheridge took him under his wing, invited him to be a part of their family dinners, shared bits of wisdom, and consistently challenged him to be the best man he could be.

Mr. Etheridge went a step further as he saw that Walter and Cynthia's relationship was heading towards marriage. He sat down with his soon-to-be son-in-law, looked him in the eyes, and said, "I believe in being a family. You don't get in this to get out of it. You get in it to stay in it." Mr. Etheridge continued, "Do you have a job? If so, where?"

That next week, Mr. Etheridge visited the place where Walter worked and watched him. Talk about intimidating! He observed his work ethic and made certain Walter was fit to provide for his daughter.

Walter passed the test, and he and his father-in-law became close friends. In one instance, Mr. Etheridge made his weekly trip to his daughter and son-in-law's home to spend some time with them. In conversation, he simply inquired about the high grass in their front yard. Walter hesitantly mentioned that he paid somebody to cut it for him because he didn't have a lawn mower at that time. Mr. Etheridge said, "Okay," and the following weekend, he showed up at the front door with a lawn mower and said, "You have no excuse to not keep the grass cut. I went and bought you a lawn mower."

That was the last time the grass got high.

Cynthia's father has since passed away, but Walter attributes much of his success and family-mindedness to his father-in-law who taught him what it means to be a man.

Walter after his interview on the "That's My Dad Podcast"

DAD STORIES

LOOKING FOR DAD IN THE STANDS

Brian and his dad

Brian Mintz - QB at Jacksonville State University

LOOKING FOR DAD IN THE STANDS

Brian Mintz

Brian Mintz grew up as a talented, multi-sport athlete. Of all the sports and all the games over the years, his dad never missed one of them. He would swap shifts with his co-workers on a regular basis, so he wouldn't have to miss his son's games, even if it meant going in extra early or staying late into the night.

Brian's success continued on the football field, and he would go on to become the quarterback at Jacksonville State University.

Today, he is 59 years old, and he vividly remembers the times, as a twenty-year-old, he would run onto the field. As the fans and student section roared and the football-field-sized band played the fight song, Brian would smile and look up to his left to the place where his parents always sat. There they were - smiling, cheering, and waving towards their son.

Most people picture this moment being something that would happen in pee-wee football or in tee-ball as a six-year-old comes to the plate for the first time; yet, here Brian is - a grown man - still longing to know that his parents were there.

It's something men never outgrow.

DAD STORIES

REUNITED WITH DAD 18 YEARS LATER

Tyler and his daughter

28

REUNITED WITH DAD
18 YEARS LATER

Tyler Hewitt

Tyler Hewitt's parents were never married, however for the first two years of his life, they both participated in his raising. When Tyler was two years old, he was living in California... until his mother strapped him into his car seat and drove 1,000 miles east to the middle-of-nowhere Texas. She didn't tell his dad that they were leaving.

In Texas, they moved in with another man who became Tyler's stepdad. While in Texas, Tyler recalls that oftentimes, they locked him in the bedroom while they used drugs. He would have to jump out of the window to go outside and play with his friends.

After a couple of years, drug issues landed both his mom and stepdad in prison, and, having nowhere to go, he moved in with some relatives of his stepdad, whom he had no relation to at all. Meanwhile, his dad was still in California searching fervently for his son, while Tyler had been coaxed into believing that his dad "skipped town" on him and wanted nothing to do with him.

Before Tyler entered the first grade, the family he was staying with packed their bags and moved to Alabama, taking Tyler with them. Once there, they lived in a tent at a campground before being approved for government housing. For the next ten years, that's where Tyler called home. He recalls having to work in the family lawn care business as a seven-year-old when, on hot days, they would only give him one 12 oz. drink per day. He cherished every sip. Although he was a kid trying his best, all he knew was spankings, groundings, and standing in the corner. As Tyler put it, "I spent much of my childhood standing in a corner." It was their way of just not having to deal with him.

As a thirteen-year-old, Tyler got into a fight with the biological son of the parents with whom he was staying. Astonishingly, they chose to press charges, and Tyler found himself locked up in a juvenile detention center. The very people he had lived with for the past several years had chosen to have him locked up.

Tyler completed the "boot camp" program and decided the detention center was better than the home he was living in, so he intentionally got himself into more trouble just so he could go back to jail. After serving his time, the authorities tried to release him back to that family, only to find out they had abandoned him.

It was then that Tyler, for the first time in his life, caught a break. He was placed at a boys' ranch - Eagle Rock Boys Home in North Alabama. After some bumps in the road, he began to excel. By this time, he was way behind in school, but the work ethic that he developed through the years of child labor helped him catch up and get his GED. When he got a job, his employer quickly noticed his hard work, his knack for running a business, and after a few years, his employer moved him into a supervisory role. Today, Tyler is one of the leaders of the company.

Tyler's story comes full circle in a beautiful way. When Tyler was twenty years old, he received a phone call from a stranger who had found him on Facebook. It was his dad. The next day, he was on a plane to meet his birth father for the very first time since the day his mom strapped him in his car seat and took him to Texas. Tyler would soon find out the true story.

His stepmother had searched for him for 18 years and finally found him. He now has a close relationship with his father and stepmother. Tyler is a role model single father to his six-year-old daughter who loves him more than anything. He's also engaged and soon to be married. All the odds were against him, yet he was able to overcome them. Generations will be better because of it.

Tyler and his daughter

DAD STORIES

PASTOR SHORTENS REVIVAL SERVICE

Norris, his wife, his son (Scott), and daughter

PASTOR SHORTENS REVIVAL SERVICE

Norris Hilton

Norris Hilton is a role model, a Christian leader, and, for many years, a well-known pastor in the community.

In the fall, their church always had a week of revival services and it was just days away. As he had done each year, Norris made it a point to schedule the revival from Monday to Thursday so that he could go watch his son, Scott, play high school football on Friday night. Well, there was a last-minute change, and on revival week Scott's football game was moved to Thursday night. What are the odds, right? Scott quickly released his parents from the obligation and pressure of missing his game and told them he fully understood that they'd have to be at the revival service.

Thursday night, the game kicked off, and Scott was playing well. At halftime, as he was heading to the locker room, he looked towards the stands mid-way up where his parents would normally have sat. To his shock, his mom and dad were there smiling and cheering.

Scott, unsure of why they were not at church, got the full story after the game. Norris had instructed the worship leader to shorten the set list for the night and, for the invitation, to only sing the first stanza. "If someone needed to get saved, they were going to have to do it in the first stanza." Then, they headed out and made it just in time for kickoff.

All these years later, Scott remains in awe of the commitment his dad showed. His pastoral ministry never took precedent over his family. Over the span of eleven years, playing sports year-round, his dad never missed a game.

DAD STORIES

DRUGS AND A FRYING PAN

Pictured left to right:
Elijah's sister, mother, Elijah, Elijah's wife, Elijah's stepdad

Sandy & Radcliff Howard
Fontaine's two children. Elijah lived with them throughout high school.

Elijah's mom - Cheryl
Elijah's mom has turned things around and made him proud

Sandra Bennett
Sandra gave Elijah a place to stay for about a year

Fontaine Howard
the mother who gave Elijah a place to call "home." He lived there with them through high school.

DRUGS and a FRYING PAN

Elijah Clark

Drugs and alcohol wreaked havoc on Elijah's childhood.

His story takes us on a roller coaster of a journey where he lived in over twenty homes with various friends and relatives before he even began high school. His overwhelming hardships began at a young age as his dad was constantly in bar fights, abusing drugs, and selling drugs. His mom had struggles of her own with mental illnesses, among other issues. Attempting to cope, she fell into an addiction to heavy drugs and would disappear for days on end, leaving seven-year-old Elijah having to take care of his little sister.

On several occasions, his parents left him and his sister locked in the vehicle outside crack houses leaving Elijah wondering if they would ever get out. Drugs and alcohol spiraled into violence which led to a divorce and forced young Elijah to move in with his uncle. Even there, drug abuse was everywhere. The dreaded cycle continued as Elijah was forced to move back in with his dad, where verbal abuse, consistent violence, and outbursts of anger were all he had ever experienced. Elijah even recalls a time his dad got mad while fishing and snapped the fishing pole over his son's leg. In another outburst, his dad pulled out his pistol and recklessly fired bullets through the walls of their home. Sadly, these types of events were commonplace.

Elijah was thrown a lifeline when a girl who lived down the street from his dad invited him to go to church with her. Elijah, desperate for hope, gave his life to Jesus Christ and began to dream of a better future. Despite his newfound faith journey, the next season continued with instability and frustration, but now, he had a different outlook on it all. He deeply hoped his dad and stepmom could find the same hope he had found. One evening in their home, Elijah boldly and lovingly told his intoxicated father that he wanted him to go to Heaven, not hell. His stepmom stepped in, twisted his words, and told his dad, "You hear that? Your son just told you to go to hell." She then cussed at Elijah, put rings on four of her fingers, reached back, and struck him across the face. Elijah, who was not even a teenager yet, stood there and took each punch saying, "Does that make you feel good hitting a kid like this?" Then, she took the frying pan sitting nearby, took her stance, and struck him with it. The force thrusted Elijah out the front door, off the porch, and into the front yard. As Elijah sprinted for safety, she began hurling rocks at him. Elijah found a safe haven in a neighbor's house and said, "My time there is done." As a fifteen-year-old, he found himself practically homeless, but his perspective was positive. His grandmother took him in and became a constant encourager for him. For the first time in his life, Elijah had a safe place to stay with someone who loved him. Tragically, his grandmother passed away not long afterwards, leaving Elijah homeless once again. From the 9th-11th grade, Elijah would "couch surf" from house to house with some friends, rarely staying in any one place very long. He was eager for the day that he would have a place to call home. Elijah's life began to shift when one particular friend from school invited him to spend a night at his house. By much of society's standards, this family was well-off. They lived in a three-story home with dozens of acres of property and three lakes. Elijah stayed two nights at their home before they realized he had been couch hopping and sleeping in a single-cab truck when a couch was not available for many months. Gutted by his journey, the husband and wife of the home sat down with him. Elijah, sitting in the very moment he had dreamed of for many years, graciously accepted their invitation to live with them. For his last two years of high school, Elijah experienced something he'd never known - a stable, healthy environment... a place he could finally call "home."

Today, Elijah's work ethic has helped him achieve a successful career. Even more importantly, he is a dedicated husband and father of two and his life's mission is to give his kids a better life than the one he had. It's largely because of the couple who took him into their home and gave him the opportunity he needed. Elijah has since forgiven his father and they have a decent relationship. His biological mother is now a committed Christian, has given up drugs, and has made Elijah proud.

Elijah and his family

DAD STORIES

A RUDE AWAKENING FOR THIS PASTOR

Keith, his wife, his children, and his son-in-law

A RUDE AWAKENING FOR
THIS PASTOR

Keith Owensby

Keith Owensby and his wife, Ashley, traveled across the southeast and evangelized for 11 years. He has been a senior pastor for the past 27 years. They have given their lives to sharing the Gospel of Jesus Christ and leading families through the tough times and the good times.

When Keith was a young pastor, he was navigating the struggles of leading a new church. The demand on him was heavy. Before he knew it, it seemed as if his life was committed fully to the church. When he came home in the evenings, he had a tough time separating the present issues at the church from home. Oftentimes, he would be physically present, but his mind was elsewhere. He would be thinking about the pressing matters of the church and tasks he needed to complete.

One afternoon, Keith zoned out while talking to Ashley. In a reality-check type of moment, she expressed her frustration and said, "If I were a regular church member, you'd listen to me."

Sadly, she was right. But, this moment shifted everything for Keith, who loves his family dearly. Today, after being a senior pastor for nearly three decades, he now makes it his top priority to be fully engaged with his family, even in seasons when the church has heavily-pressing matters. He has learned to be a great listener and never to let pastoral ministry cause him to neglect his family.

Kenneth and his dad

32

YOUR DAD DID WHAT?!

Kenneth Bruce

For Kenneth, there was one moment that stands out among many others where his dad impressed him beyond measure.

Kenneth was a gifted athlete, and he achieved great success on the soccer field in high school.

While Kenneth was growing up near Lexington, Kentucky, his dad was living his dream as the Public Address Announcer for the University of Kentucky's basketball and football games. This was a big deal in the sports world.

When Kenneth entered high school, his games were typically on Saturdays. His dad deeply loved being present at his games to watch him play and was forced to make a decision, one that many would view as difficult. There were only two options: he could go watch his son's soccer games on Saturdays, or he could continue to live his dream working for UK Athletics. For Kenneth's dad, there was only one option. He chose to give up his dream so he could watch his son play soccer - a decision that still leaves his son awestruck.

Today, more than twenty years later, Kenneth is still moved by what his dad did just to watch him play. Using the many glimpses of commitment and sacrifice he saw in his dad as the standard, Kenneth now models that to his children. He and his wife, Kristy, have five children: Noah, Adoniram, Asa, Nathan, and Ellie Ann.

DAD STORIES

YOU HAVE BABE RUTH'S AUTOGRAPH?!

Ric and his wife, Carla

YOU HAVE BABE RUTH'S AUTOGRAPH?!

Ric Callahan

"You have Babe Ruth's autograph?!"

Ric's buddy was an avid Babe Ruth fan and collected his cards, memorabilia, and studied much of his story and statistics. Ric needed some extra money and saw an opportunity.

Ric told his buddy that he had a baseball at home that had Babe Ruth's autograph on it. "I'll sell it to you for $10." Recognizing the beauty of the deal and overwhelmed at the thought of having such a treasured item, his friend quickly said, "I have $10!"

Ric headed home, grabbed one of the balls they threw around, picked up a pen, and forged Babe Ruth's autograph between the seams. With the "signed" ball in hand, he met back up with his buddy to reveal the coveted piece of baseball history.

His friend was elated. Ric was elated! They finalized the transaction. It was a win/win for everyone! But, Ric made one dreadful mistake that cost him this fortune. Later that evening, Ric's dad got a phone call. It was Ric's buddy's dad letting him know about the situation. Hilariously, Ric had used a "Dixie Youth" baseball to forge the autograph.

Together, he and Ric went directly over to his buddy's house where Ric was forced to apologize, return the $10, and even had to let his friend keep the baseball. Talk about a lose/lose/lose.

Although it's a funny laugh now, it was a powerful lesson of integrity and honesty for a young boy.

DAD STORIES

Vista (right), his wife, daughter, and the couple he now considers his parents. The man on the left is the only dad he's ever known.

DAD KILLED SEVEN PEOPLE

Vista McDuffie

Vista grew up living with his mother and his stepdad. His biological dad killed seven people, and as a result, spent the large majority of Vista's life in prison. His stepdad was a "raging drug addict." They even went without power on many occasions because all the money was spent on drugs.

When Vista was just a child, his mom and stepdad would leave him at home alone while they went to rob local jewelry stores. Many times, they would leave Vista by himself for days at a time without food. Vista, only a child, would walk down the street to the local grocery store and stuff Hot Pockets into his jacket and walk out of the store with them. Then, he would run an extension chord to the outlet outside his neighbor's house, so he could plug in the microwave and heat up his hot pocket. This happened dozens of times.

A neighbor saw the instability and neglect that was present in Vista's home and snuck him a key to their house. They wanted him to have a safe place to go in a moment of crisis. He now considers this couple to be "family."

Vista has only seen his biological dad four or five times in his life. Despite his dad's actions, Vista still wanted to have a relationship with him. His biological dad had a genius mind but just used it for the wrong things. He escaped from prison several times. When he would escape, he would come to pick up Vista and Vista's mom, and they would get away until the authorities found him again.

When Vista was fourteen years old, his biological dad called him from prison and asked him to do him a favor. He wanted Vista to sneak a joint in through his belt when visitation hours opened. Vista replied, "You don't care anything about me." It was at this point that Vista chose to never have anything else to do with him.

As a young man, Vista drifted into a life of crime. He began to fall victim to the same cycle - the only one he had ever known. During a car theft one night, he narrowly escaped before the police got to him. This proved to be a moment of awakening as he saw how close he was to being locked up just like his dad. After some deep contemplation and asking himself some hard questions, Vista made the decision that his life would look different. It was not long before he joined the military and served for twenty-five years.

Today, Vista is an honorable man.

When he had no model, there was a group of men that stepped up and took Vista under their wing. They invested in him, taught him what it means to be a man and showed him how to be a great dad. He credits their sacrifice and love for why he is not locked up today like his father.

Vista, his wife, and daughter

DAD STORIES

TWO SONS AND A SWORD

Cris and his two sons

TWO SONS AND A SWORD

Cris Mahy

As Cris' sons, Nathan and Jordan, reached their senior year of high school, Cris wanted to create a special event that would impact them and prepare them for manhood. He wanted to give them something that would help them see the significance of the season and hold them accountable to the magnitude of their responsibility as men - a "rite of passage," if you will. He decided to plan a special night for his two sons.

As graduation day was approaching, he asked seven of the men who had played a vital role in his sons' lives to give him a list of the five most impactful books they had read. For each one, he organized a gathering where these men would have the opportunity to speak to each of his sons and pray over them.

When the anticipated night came, Cris gave both his boys a chest filled with multiple books that his friends had recommended, shared his heart with them, prayed over them, and blessed them. Before the night ended, he pulled out one final gift - a William Wallace type sword. On the sword, their favorite Bible verse was engraved, along with their name and the date the sword was presented.

This special night is one that is penned into each of their hearts and minds. Even to this day, some twenty years later, his sons are still moved by the memory of the night their father charged them to go forward and fulfill God's purpose in their lives.

The sword is a sharp and powerful reminder that there are things worth battling for! It's a charge to never stop fighting for family.

DAD STORIES

SLEEPWALKING AND LOOKING FOR DAD

Jerome's mom and dad

AUG 1959

36

SLEEPWALKING AND LOOKING FOR DAD

Jerome Thomas

Jerome's dad died suddenly when he was six years old. In addition to that, his mom dealt with physical limitations and was confined to a wheelchair. As the oldest sibling, he became the man of the house. The sudden loss of his dad wreaked havoc on Jerome in ways that are still tough to talk about.

He went from being a calm kid in a safe environment to an angry kid trapped in the effects of trauma. He carried this anger for many years and would have outbursts of rage. He began to sleepwalk, often waking up in different parts of the house. Once, he walked out of the front door and went house to house asking neighbors where his dad was. The trauma was intense.

Jerome loved his dad dearly. Some fifty years later, he still recalls vivid memories he and his dad had shared. His dad did not laugh in some of these moments, but young Jerome got a kick of out them.

Jerome remembers climbing in the driver's seat of his dad's big truck where he would pull the air horn and laugh at his dad's startled reaction. Once, while in the truck, he accidentally bumped the hand brake. As the truck began to roll, accelerating toward the edge of a cliff on their property, his dad sprinted and caught up with the vehicle. He dove through the driver's side window to re-engage the brake. Jerome was only six at the time but has fond memories of these times he spent with his dad.

As a young adult, Jerome crossed paths with some men in his church who committed time to mentor him. Jerome often gets emotional thinking about the impact these men had on his life. They filled the gap. They stepped in and made the difference by investing intentionally into Jerome's life. Through much prayer and guidance, God began to give him a new perspective. The rage he had carried in his heart for many years began to shift into a burning compassion for hurting children. God was calling him to be a father figure to boys who were trapped in trauma's grip and unsure how to move forward. Today, Jerome has answered that call with a resounding "Yes." He leads a mentoring ministry and serves on the Board of Eagle Rock Boys Home where he has volunteered his time for nearly three decades, investing in the lives of boys who were raised in homes where the father was often absent or abusive.

God continues to use the difficulties of his personal journey as a platform to serve others and share the Gospel of Jesus Christ.

Jerome and his wife

DAD STORIES

WAR HEROES REUNITED

Mike with Scott after he shared his dad's story on the "That's My Dad Podcast."

37

WAR HEROES REUNITED

Mike Davis

Mike's dad, Coy, was a professional baseball player in the 1950s before being drafted into military service to fight in the Korean War. As a member of the famous 7th Infantry Division, Coy and eight of his buddies were on a surveillance mission when a bomb exploded. He was particularly close to one of the eight guys; they were very good friends.

Miraculously, he survived the explosion but was taken to a different trauma unit than his friend. During the long road of recovery, he just assumed his buddy had been killed in the field that afternoon. Telephones were not easily accessible in the 1950s. He could not just pick up a phone to check on him and fearing the worst, decided not to try.

For nearly five decades, Coy avoided the thought of it. In the 1990s, nearly fifty years later, he received a phone call from a man who had tracked him down. It was his buddy from the 7th Infantry Division. In a beautiful reunification, they met and tried to make up for lost time. They stayed in touch and have built a wonderful friendship.

The story comes full circle a little later when all nine of the men in that 7th Infantry Division were reunited. Nearly five decades after the incident, they were all still living. Each one dealt with post-war trauma; however, against all odds, all of them were still married to their first wife, living a life of humility and sacrifice, and leading their family well.

For Mike, this story is living proof that even if we are given a tough hand, we can choose how we will respond.

The resolve Mike's dad exhibited to push through the post-war issues he was dealing with and stay faithful and committed to his wife and family have paid massive dividends today as Mike, his kids, and his grandkids are all walking the same path - faithful, committed, and honorable.

Mike often says of his dad, "If I can be half the person he's been, I will be successful."

Mike and his dad, Coy

DAD STORIES

Walter and his wife, Cynthia

DAD LIVED DOWN THE STREET
NOBODY TOLD ME

Walter Smith

Walter Smith was raised without a father. Growing up, he always wondered about his dad and would occasionally hear stories about him and what he was like. Throughout elementary, middle, and much of high school, he watched all of his friends interact with their dads and dreamed about what that could be like with his dad. When completing contact information for school forms or providing a copy of his birth certificate for various needs, the void would flare. As with all fatherless kids, there was an ache deep within his heart.

Walter was 18 years old when he finally met his dad. It began at the local barber shop where he struck up a conversation with a gentleman who he soon learned was his uncle - his dad's brother. Through this new connection, Walter was able to meet his dad for the first time. Although their first interaction was slightly awkward, it was a milestone moment for Walter.

As Walter was trying to put the pieces together, he discovered that his dad had lived just down the road all this time. For 18 years, he had been minutes from his dad and nobody ever told him.

"This was crushing. Heartbreaking."

Naturally, Walter began to question everything.

"Why didn't Mom tell me?"
"Why didn't my grandparents tell me?"
"Why didn't anyone tell me?"

Resentment began to build towards everyone and then reached a breaking point where the frustration and hurt were destroying him. His aunt approached him and had a straightforward, no-nonsense conversation with him. "You have to let this go. It's doing more damage to you than it is to them."

Walter, recognizing the toll it was taking on him, adhered to this life-changing advice and began his journey to forgiveness and healing. During the years he was in college, he was able to spend some time with his dad, and they built a relationship together. Tragically, Walter's dad was struck by a car while walking across the street which put him in a nursing home, where he would eventually pass away.

Those days sitting next to his dad's bedside are some of the most precious to Walter. Before his dad passed, in a full-circle, monumental moment, Walter was given the opportunity to lead his father to Jesus Christ.

"That's the greatest gift any man can receive. That was special to me. Even though my father never gave me any natural gifts, my Heavenly Father gave my dad the gift of eternal life. That was the greatest gift to me."

Walter and Scott after Walter's interview on the "That's My Dad Podcast"

DAD STORIES

FIVE GENERATIONS OF GODLY FATHERS

James and his dad

39

FIVE GENERATIONS OF
GODLY FATHERS

James Pullen

James Pullen is the father of five talented and ultra-successful adult children. Impressively, each have achieved great success in academics, business, and in life. James often jokes that his kids' success is evidence that the apple can, indeed, fall far from the tree.

The natural question that arises is: What can a father do to raise children who are kind, successful, and well-respected?

It began decades prior with James' grandfather. His grandfather lost his dad when he was three years old. He started working at the Steel Mill when he was only fourteen years old to help provide for his family. Although he was too young to remember much about his dad, he worked hard and figured out how to be a great man. Many obstacles stood in his way as he embarked on this journey to becoming a great man, but he persevered. Now, over 100 years later, what has happened is astonishing. He paved the way for, now, five generations of Godly men to live productive lives by embracing a good work ethic, a love for family, and making a sacrifice for the betterment of others.

James and his wife place a huge emphasis on surrounding their kids with the right kind of people. Their faith family became their kids' support system and was a strength and comfort to them in different seasons of life.

In addition, James and his wife have taken their kids on international mission trips to expose them to different cultures and teach them the importance of serving. They give of themselves on these trips but always receive more than they are able to give. Incredibly, James simply sees himself as an average dad just doing the small things the right way. Maybe that is what it is about, though. Maybe it is less about doing extraordinary things and more about doing the small things the right way over a long period of time.

If you want to raise successful kids, take a note from James' playbook.

James with his wife and family

DAD STORIES

CALLED MY 78-YEAR-OLD DAD ABOUT A BOAT

Mark (standing far right), his brother, sister, mom, and dad

CALLED MY 78-YEAR-OLD DAD ABOUT A BOAT

Mark Price

As Mark was growing up, he and his dad had a special bond. His dad was intentional about instilling in his son what he needed to live a productive life and lead his family well. Now, Mark is in his fifties and his dad is seventy-eight years old. Although seasons have changed over the years, one aspect has not. Mark still prioritizes calling his dad.

Sometimes, it's just to talk. Other times, it's to tell him about something that took place that day. Often times, it is to ask his dad for advice. Not long ago, he needed some help with a boat trailer he had purchased, so he called his dad and asked for advice on how to fix it. This simple gesture meant the world to his dad.

No matter how old you are, give your dad a call if you still have him.

Make it happen often. It may just mean the world to him.

DAD STORIES

THE HAMBY FAMILY PLAN

Blake, his wife, and their two kids

The Hamby Family Plan that still hangs in their kitchen

THE HAMBY FAMILY PLAN

Blake Hamby

Blake Hamby did something while on an anniversary trip with his wife that shifted the course of his family and home.

Before he and his wife, Erin, embarked on their anniversary trip, he took the time to prepare a detailed PowerPoint presentation to map out what God had been doing in his heart - how he needed to lead his family, what areas his family needed to improve, and where they needed to focus.

While they were in their hotel room one evening, Blake presented this "family overhaul" of sorts to his wife - with an intense focus on growing together as a family.

Without hesitation, Erin jumped on board. This fresh vision has taken their family to another level. They have developed a Family Mission Statement, Family Disciplines, Family Values, Family Verse, and a Family Prayer. When they got back home and rejoined their two daughters, Blake had their new Family Plan written out on a beautiful piece of wood and placed on the wall in their kitchen. Today, it still hangs there as a reminder to steward well what they have been given.

Maybe some dads out there need to take the time to survey their homes and see what changes need to be made so their homes can go to another level. Go ahead. While you are at it, make a PowerPoint presentation and share it with your wife. It might just make all the difference.

DAD STORIES

DAD DIDN'T GIVE UP ON ME

Jacob, his wife, and their two children

42

DAD DIDN'T GIVE UP ON ME

Jacob Graul

Jacob Graul's biological father abandoned him at birth and has never had a relationship with him. His birth mother was sick most of his life and recently passed away. However, he had a great stepdad who loved him as his own. Jacob shares how his stepdad, whom he refers to as "dad," came from a difficult personal upbringing but somehow taught himself to be a great father so he could create a good life for Jacob and his brother. Despite his dad's efforts, Jacob's childhood was filled with rebellion. At one point, he was placed in a behavioral treatment center in an effort to change the trajectory of his life.

As a senior in high school, his rebellion took a turn for the worse. He and his friend thought it would be funny to get drunk one day before school, so they did. As a result, he was expelled from school only a few weeks before graduation. He was forced to attend an alternative school program to finish school and get his diploma.

Jacob stood at a crossroad moment. After a lot of self-reflection, and realizing how many people he had let down in his life, he was ready to make a change. He told his dad that he didn't want to live like this. His dad, who had a brother who had spent many years in jail, told him he was headed down the same path, but it was not too late to turn things around. It's a statement that remains on the forefront of Jacob's mind still today - some ten years later. Jacob joined the military, worked several jobs along the way and, today is a successful real-estate developer.

When he reflects on what life could have been had he stayed on the course he was on, Jacob is grateful. He is grateful for friends and mentors like Steve, who never gave up on him when everyone else did. He is grateful for the teachers that thought he would never amount to anything because it fueled his desire to change his life. He is thankful for that defining moment in the living room where his dad reminded him that it was not too late.

Today, Jacob is a faithful husband and a father of two. Every day, he is thankful for those who didn't give up on him.

Jacob, his son, and his newborn daughter

DAD STORIES

ABANDONED AT AGE 7

James and his mom

43

ABANDONED AT AGE 7

James Spann

James' dad abandoned him when he was five years old. He literally walked out one night and never came back. To know James Spann today, one would never know it. He's a nationally-renowned, award-winning Meteorologist whose voice is front and center during dangerous storms. The ache of his father abandoning him is one he still feels today - some sixty years later.

It was just him and his mom. They "were dying on the inside." James went into a shell, didn't trust people, and didn't want to interact with people. He and his mother had to work hard just to survive because his dad never paid any child support. Not even eight years old, he was cutting grass to try and help his mom make ends meet.

Things began to slowly shift when James and his mom moved to Tuscaloosa. There were people who stepped in and came alongside them, easing the aching and giving them a glimpse of a better future. The principal of the school knew James' back story and would step in and say things like, "You look good today" and "I believe in you." Against everything he felt in his heart, he started taking the principal's word for it. With each compliment and each encouragement, hope was slowly being reborn in his heart. When James was twelve years old, he committed his life to Jesus Christ. Years later, he was doing life with a community of men who were acquainted with his upbringing, and they encouraged him to pray this prayer: "Open my eyes and open my ears to the needs of the people around me."

The next day, God began to burn something new in his heart. He was overwhelmingly compelled by the thought that he needed to help his dad.

He began to research to see if his dad was even still alive. He was, indeed, and to his surprise, was living only a few hours north. He and his buddy hopped in the car, headed north, and spent all day knocking on doors asking if anybody knew him. Finally, somebody told them where he lived. When the door opened, James was looking at his father for the first time in 30 years.

At that moment, memories flooded back to his mind of times he and his dad spent together before he abandoned them - afternoons fishing together, a night at the circus, and others. He remembered all of this vividly from when he was 5 or 6 years old. After a few moments of introduction and conversation, James looked at his father and began to share the Gospel with him, only to be verbally rejected in return. His dad cussed both him and his friend, then walked out to the front yard and urinated twice while James continued to share about Jesus. He would later learn that his dad was suffering from alcohol dementia - a condition that was a result of chronic alcohol abuse for years. It wasn't long after this interaction that his dad passed away. Nobody wanted to deal with a funeral, so James took initiative and had his body cremated. After the cremation, James took his ashes and began the drive toward the family cemetery to sprinkle them. It was on this drive that he began to get the healing he needed.

While he was driving there, he felt the overwhelming need to voice his forgiveness. So, that's what he did. "I forgive you. I forgive you." He said it over and over. Then, he began to voice his gratitude for his dad. He thanked him for taking him fishing and for taking him to the circus. It's a moment that won't make sense to most, but it was a monumental moment in his life as he solidified his forgiveness and was sure to finish well. To this day, he clings to the hope that his dad loved him.

Today, James visits elementary schools and high schools across the state of Alabama several times a week. He does not get paid a dime to do it but has given much of his life to investing in young kids, many of whom are being raised much like he was. He remembers the impact that the principal's actions had on him in a desperate season and aims to make the same difference in the lives of many others. He's doing just that.

James and Scott after the interview on the That's My Dad Podcast

DAD STORIES

NO IDEA HOW DAD PULLED THAT OFF

Rene, his two sons, and his dad – "Coach Z"

Rene, his brother Kaleb, and "Coach Z"

44

NO IDEA HOW DAD
PULLED THAT OFF

Rene Zeringue

Rene Zeringue was raised in a great home with loving parents. His dad modeled what it meant to be a great dad - selfless, committed, and sacrificial. His dad was, and still is, a very intelligent man, which afforded him some high-level opportunities in the workspace that required much of him. He traveled often, and had to work a lot of hours, but he somehow found a way to always be present with his two sons.

Oftentimes, he'd come to their practices or be at their games, then have to go back to work for several hours after it ended. Whatever it took, he was going to be there. Each year, he found a way to coach his sons, which all of his sons' friends loved. "Coach Z" became a father figure to many of those young boys. Some, through no fault of their own, didn't have a father in their homes.

Through all of his dads' responsibilities, it was never unclear how great his dad's love for them was. His consistency, diligence, commitment, and sacrifice proved it, and continues to prove it, each day.

Now a grown man with five kids of his own, Rene often thinks back on how his dad managed his workload without neglecting his family. He still cannot figure it out. He has no idea how his dad pulled it off.

DAD STORIES

A FRUSTRATING HOME LIFE AND A RUNAWAY CHILD

Dr. Mike and his family with his mom

A FRUSTRATING HOME LIFE AND A RUNAWAY CHILD

Mike McClellan

Mike McClellan was just three weeks old when his dad passed away. A year later, his mother remarried, and her new husband adopted Mike. His name was Jim. Jim was one of 13 children and was raised by an alcoholic father. His home was very unstable, and violence was a common element. Jim found himself trapped in the only cycle he had ever known.

Mike's life became very unpredictable, and alcohol was reaping devastating effects in their home. In one instance, Jim grabbed Mike's mom, pinned her against the wall, grabbed her by the throat and clenched his fist to punch her. Mike quickly jumped in between the two of them, grabbed Jim by the throat, and clenched his fist. There, they stood. After a few moments of looking eye-to-eye, Jim bowed out and ran upstairs, but that's when things took another turn. Mike's mom stepped in and said to her son, "You need to go apologize to him." This became very evident to Mike how Jim's generational curse began to affect the entire family.

To escape the turmoil, Mike once ran away from home with his friend as a 15-year-old. They hitch-hiked their way from town to town until, finally, after a week had gone by, they ran out of money. Running out of options, they turned themselves in to the police, so they could get in touch with their parents. After a night at the police station, Mike's parents arrived to pick him up. Once in the car, Jim asked, "Did you run out of money?" Mike said, "Yes," and Jim threw a twenty-dollar bill in his lap and said, "Do you want to keep going?" Mike knew this had really upset his mother, so he decided to return home.

As a young man, Mike vowed to himself that he was going to turn it around and be the dad to his kids that he never had. All these years later, he has held to that commitment beautifully. Today, he and his wife are renowned chiropractors with a successful business. They are heavily involved in serving their community and are making positive impacts on many young people. More importantly, Mike is the hero to his wife and two adult children, who are now having success of their own. His story proves that regardless of how difficult your background is, you can indeed flip the script on your family tree.

Dr. Mike, his wife, and two children

ON THE JOB TRAINING

DAD STORIES

Kenneth (left) , his son (right), and two grandsons (middle)

46

ON THE JOB TRAINING

Kenneth Malone

For the majority of Kenneth's childhood and teenage years, his biological father was not involved in his life. His parents had divorced then his dad remarried, had children, and moved out of state.

His mom also remarried and Kenneth was raised by his mom and stepdad. Tragically, his stepdad was abusive. This abuse created a toxic environment and many years of instability in their home. Kenneth wasn't allowed to invite friends over and things were always tense. Despite this, Kenneth just "made do."

While Kenneth was playing basketball with some friends at the local gym, one of his friends introduced him to a man who looked a lot like him. As they stood and shook hands, he realized he had just met his brother for the first time. He had known his brother existed, but had never known who he was.

Through this connection with his brother, Kenneth was able to meet his biological dad, who had moved back to Atlanta. During this season, Kenneth made a commitment. Although he carried bitterness and hurt because his dad abandoned him, he vowed to himself that if his dad was willing to have a relationship with him, he'd do everything he could to make it happen.

Turns out, at a beautiful turning point, Kenneth and his dad began to build a relationship. Kenneth soon learned that his dad had many regrets. When he found out his dad wished he'd done things differently, it was an important step in Kenneth's healing process. Today, they have a great relationship. When it became time for Kenneth to be a dad, himself, it was on-the-job training. Clearly, he didn't have an example. Although he's made some mistakes, as every dad has, he's committed each day to love his kids. Instead of being angry, he's determined to make it better for his kids.

Today, his kids will be the first to tell you that he's done just that. He's flipped the script.

Kenneth and Scott after the interview on the "That's My Dad Podcast"

DAD STORIES

DAD WOKE ME UP AT THE FRAT HOUSE

Mark and Scott after the interview on the "That's My Dad Podcast"

DAD WOKE ME UP AT
THE FRAT HOUSE

Mark Price

When Mark Price was in college as a 19-year-old, he made some poor decisions. One night, he had been drinking at the frat house with some of his buddies and made the wise decision to stay the night there instead of driving home. However, he failed to communicate this with his dad, whom he had promised to help mow the yard first thing the next morning.

The next morning came and Mark was nowhere to be found. His dad showed up at the frat house looking for him. "Has anyone seen Mark?" Knowing the situation and how early it was in the morning, one of his buddies ran to where Mark was sleeping, woke him up, and said, "Yo, your dad is looking for you." Mark, still half asleep, obliviously replied, "Tell him I'll call him back in a minute."

The friend said, "He's downstairs."

Looking at the clock and realizing he had forgotten about the yard, Mark quickly hopped up and ran downstairs.

His dad, recognizing what had happened the night before, reminded his son of the commitment he had made to cutting the grass. Mark, thinking he was getting off easy, told his dad he would be home in a few minutes. His dad replied, "No, son. You're coming home right now. If you're gonna be a man at night, you're gonna be a man in the morning."

Mark immediately went home and cut the grass.
His dad taught him a powerful lesson on integrity that morning by holding his son to his word. It's a lesson Mark still clings to today.

DAD STORIES

EXPOSURE EXPANDS EXPECTATION

Ty and his mom

Ty cutting hair

Ty and his Pastor

EXPOSURE EXPANDS EXPECTATION

Ty Dillon

Ty Dillon was born in Louisiana and raised in Milwaukee, Wisconsin in a fatherless home. Standing in line to get food and not having the best clothes or shoes was Ty's reality despite the hard work of his mom to try to make ends meet. Walking through the snow to get to school in Milwaukee, Wisconsin, was just the way it had to be. As a child, it was normal. It was life.

It was only him and his mom. He knew his Dad was not in the picture but never questioned why. Later in life, he learned that his mom and dad were never married and their relationship wasn't working, so his mom decided to leave and his dad chose not to follow. Growing up without that male role model, Ty began to recognize that his friends who had their dads knew things he didn't. They knew how to work on cars and shoot pool, but Ty just stood there confused. He knew something was off. He didn't have anyone to teach him those types of things.

Through his teenage years, he began to intentionally observe different men to put together a hodge-podge dad of sorts. He would observe that one man spent time with his family, one man had an awesome job, and one man was fit and athletic. Then, he would aim to become a combination of the good traits of these men. Brilliantly, this was how Ty learned to become a great man.

Along the way, other men stepped in, and he would intently listen and learn, absorbing any piece of wisdom he could. As an up-and-coming barber in Milwaukee, Ty got the opportunity to work at a well-known barber shop there. The business owner took him under his wing and taught him business structure, financial stewardship, and how to properly interact with customers. This was just another person that God had placed in Ty's life to help fill the void.

Ty's Pastor, who has been a father figure in his life since his adult years, told him a statement that shook his whole perspective on life: "Exposure Expands Expectation." Ty learned that, in order to see what is possible, he had to get outside the confinement of what he had known in his childhood. His aim is to do that today with the kids and young men he invests in. He and his wife often take them shopping and to restaurants they normally could not afford. He is a believer that, if they can be exposed to better, they will not settle for less.

Day in and day out, Ty is applying this to his own family. His mission in life is to give his kids what he didn't have - a home where the father was present and actively engaged in their lives. When asked what he hopes his kids will say about him one day, he replied, "That he loved them beyond words."

Ty, his wife, and his children

DAD STORIES

THE GREATEST MEMORY I HAVE WITH MY DAD

Eddie and his wife

THE GREATEST MEMORY I HAVE
WITH MY DAD

Eddie Nichols

Eddie's father was a traveling salesman, so he was not at home as much as he would have liked while Eddie was growing up. However, he was a provider, taught his children the importance of work ethic, and genuinely loved them. Because he was gone a lot, Eddie and his dad didn't have a super close relationship. They loved each other and treated each other with respect, but they didn't have too many vulnerable conversations.

In 1969, out of nowhere, Eddie's dad planned a big surprise for his son. Early in the morning, they loaded up the car and headed towards Atlanta where Tom Seaver and the Mets were taking on Phil Neikro and the Braves in the NLCS. In an act well outside of "the norm," his dad had put together this special day for him and his son to share together. They cheered on the Braves and enjoyed the historic game. But, the day wasn't over.

They hopped back in the vehicle in Atlanta, and his dad had another surprise up his sleeve. They began the three-hour drive to Tuscaloosa, Alabama. When they arrived at Bryant-Denny Stadium, Eddie couldn't believe it. Archie Manning and the Ole Miss Rebels were playing Scott Hunter and the Alabama Crimson Tide. Together, they cheered on their favorite team. While the game was going on, Eddie noticed that his dad was speaking to him more, which was unusual. His dad was normally quiet, focused on work, and distant. But, not this day.

After eight hours on the road and two historic games in two different states, they arrived home a little after midnight. It's a day that Eddie, fifty-four years later, still cherishes. As he puts it, "It's the greatest memory I have with my dad."

DAD STORIES

A STORY OF REDEMPTION

Mike and his family

50

A STORY OF REDEMPTION

Mike Wilcut

One who knows Mike Wilcut would assume he grew up in a model, traditional family that never had any problems. He is a highly respected professional, a role model in the community, a church leader, and a father to four successful children. However, his journey was anything but easy.

While he was growing up, his father had a serious problem with alcohol. Oftentimes, the alcoholism turned into intense moments where his father would beat his mother. This continued off and on for much of Mike's childhood and teenage years.

One afternoon, the violence began to surface again. Mike was a grown man at this point and had moved out of the house. Mike's mom frantically called Mike as his dad had become belligerent and violent. Mike hurried over to the house, stepped inside and demanded that it stop now. Inches from his dad's face with his finger in his chest, Mike said, "Don't you ever ever do that again or there will be consequences." Incredibly, it never happened again.

As time went on, Mike's dad was growing more and more desperate for a better way of living. In a miraculous turn of events, he turned to Jesus Christ. His life underwent a massive transformation, which equipped him to give up alcohol altogether. Over time, his dad learned to love his mom, protect her, and care for her. He and his dad also mended their relationship. What a beautiful story of redemption!

Today, Mike has put the pieces of the puzzle together. His dad was raised in a rough home with rough parents who were not examples of the right way to live. His life had been a struggle. He had no role model. He desperately needed someone to set the standard and teach him how to uphold it. Without that standard before him, he continued in the only way he had known.

This generational mindset stopped with Mike. Through intentional choices and a long-term commitment to a better way of living, the cycle was broken. His four children have been raised to embrace family and are raising their kids the very same way.

Mike with Scott after his interview on the "That's My Dad Podcast."

DAD STORIES

FORGIVING MOM AND STEPDAD

Dustin, his mom, and his stepdad

FORGIVING MOM & STEPDAD

Dustin Freeman

Dustin Freeman's parents divorced when he was only two years old. He lived the next ten years with his mother and stepfather, but sadly, it was not a pleasant ten years.

Alcohol began to cause major problems in their home. Dustin often took the brunt of the drinking when his mom and stepdad would lash out at him. On the weekends that Dustin was with his dad and stepmom, he was exposed to a different lifestyle. They went to church, spent quality time together and learned what it meant to have a stable household. However, he still struggled greatly because he knew his mom loved him and he loved his mom dearly. As the tension continued to build, it reached a breaking point when Dustin was twelve years old.

With the instability and struggle of being in the home with his mom and stepdad, he asked a judge to allow him to move into his father's home. His wish was granted, and Dustin spent the rest of his youth with his dad. Living with his dad, Dustin continued to gain great respect for him. His dad was one who would apologize when he was wrong or when he spoke in a harsh tone, which caused Dustin's love for him to continue to grow. His dad was a man of his word and taught Dustin the importance of integrity. He had never had a close relationship with someone like this.

Incredibly, there came another turning point in his life. After carrying frustration and resentment towards his mom and stepdad and being unable to move forward from it totally for quite some time, Dustin's first daughter was born.

When she was born, Dustin had a shift in his heart and began to long for the day where his mom and stepdad could be present in his little girl's life.

After several vulnerable conversations and authentic apologies, Dustin, his mom, and stepdad began the journey to making amends. In a beautiful full-circle moment, they continue to have a great relationship today. They are loving and caring grandparents, and Dustin and his wife fully trust them.

Today, Dustin is the Director of the Independent Living Program at Eagle Rock Boys Home where he is giving his life to help older teenage boys prepare for their journey on their own. His story is a message of hope. Even if it feels like it's too far gone, it's not too late.

Dustin, his wife, and their two children

DAD STORIES

FIRST TIME HEARING, "SON, I LOVE YOU"

Taylor Gallman

Taylor, his dad Andy, and their family

FIRST TIME HEARING "SON, I LOVE YOU"

Taylor Gallman

Taylor and his dad, Andy, had a tense relationship, to say the least. Taylor had undiagnosed dyslexia and was thought to be the misfit of the family as he struggled through school, struggled in social realms, and didn't interact with others as well as his siblings. His dad, an intelligent and successful man, treated him differently than his other children. Andy was distant, disengaged, and didn't seem to want anything to do with his son. Taylor would go to his dad and say, "I love ya, Dad." His dad would reply, "Yeah, me too." His dad couldn't tell him he loved him and Taylor didn't understand why. Over the years, resentment settled in and grew fiercely, causing reconciliation to seem like an ever-growing impossibility. This relational strain endured for eighteen years until one moment changed it all.

When Taylor was eighteen years old, he finally mustered up the strength to walk into his dad's room and address the years of tension. He said, "Dad, I don't know why you hate me." Andy looked at his son, and to Taylor's disbelief, broke into tears. Andy said, "I don't hate you. I just don't understand you." In this life-altering moment, Taylor broke down in tears, as well. For the first time, they both humbly agreed they had both made great mistakes. Andy recognized that he had spent 18 years counting off his son as "stupid" and "a misfit," while Taylor admitted he had allowed the tension and mistreatment to create further division between them. Taylor believed his dad hated him when, in reality, he never did. He had never been taught how to deal with a son who was not like him and his other children.

As they began to mend their relationship, Taylor still remembers the moment when he walked into his dad's house, sat down with him, and said, "Dad, I love you." Andy looked back at his son and said, "Son, I love you too." It's a moment Taylor still gets emotional about today. He and his dad went on and became the best of friends.

When Taylor had children of his own, he vowed that they would never go a day without knowing their father loved them with all his heart. It is a vow that, all these years later, he has kept with all four of his children.

Taylor and his family

DAD STORIES

ABUSED. NEGLECTED. WOULDN'T CHANGE IT.

James Kelly

James with his parents - Andy & Belinda Hiti - and his family

ABUSED. NEGLECTED.
WOULDN'T CHANGE IT

James Kelley

James' mother died when he was five. He lived with his biological father for 5 years. James describes the 5 years as "the worst." After several very difficult years of abuse and neglect, he and his brother moved in with their aunt hoping that things would get better. They didn't. It was the same ole story of abuse and violence.

The Department of Human Resources took James and his brother away from his aunt when James was 12 years old, and they entered the foster system. After experiencing multiple foster care placements, both James and his brother were placed at Eagle Rock - the boys home where they would spend the rest of their teenage years.

Growing up, James was eager for the day when he could be a part of a loving family. He'd sit outside and dream about having someone to love and experience life with. Landing at the Eagle Rock Boys Home was a turning point in James' life as it was there that James began to learn the value of hard work and being teachable. With a laugh, he said that he quickly figured out, "If you'll just work hard, people will pay you."

When James was 15 years old and on his journey of healing, a couple - Andy and Belinda Hiti - joined the mission of Eagle Rock Boys Home to pour into the boys. James was one of those boys. As James put it, "Andy was the one who taught me that it was okay to be gentle." For context, Andy is a strong firefighter standing 6'4, but beautifully models gentleness and kindness. The impact Andy and Belinda were having on James was massive and James knew it.

When James graduated from high school, he continued to build his relationship with Andy, Belinda, and their family. They became his resource parents and, often, what was supposed to be one night at their home became multiple nights. James was slowly taking more clothes over there. This led to that moment James had dreamed of for many years. Andy and Belinda expressed their desire to adopt James and make him an official part of their family. In this special moment, James replied, "Absolutely."

For the first time in his life, James had a stable, healthy family to call his own. He didn't have to dream anymore; it was now his reality. When James was asked if he'd go back and rewrite his journey, his reply revealed how far he'd come.

"Maybe if you'd asked me if I was a kid, absolutely. But with who I turned out to be - my life story made me who I am." He continued, "If I rewrote the story and had a normal childhood, I wouldn't have these experiences and look at life the way I do now."

Tragically, James' older brother, Raymond, was killed in a car accident at the age of 19. This left James without the only person who had shared his difficult life experiences, but James' story didn't end there.

Today, he is a faithful husband and father and excels greatly in his career. All the odds were against him. He faced adversity beyond belief. Yet, today, his unwavering commitment to his wife and kids has shifted the trajectory of the generations that will follow him.

James with his wife and their two children

DAD STORIES

A FATHER'S BELIEF IN HIS SON

Ty with a tiger and a black bear at his wildlife sanctuary

A FATHER'S BELIEF
IN HIS SON

Ty Harris

When Ty Harris was asked what stood out most about his dad, he said, "My dad instilled within me an attitude of 'You can accomplish anything you want to accomplish if you're willing to work for it.'" Growing up hearing this, Ty had no idea the impact it would have on him as life continued.

Ty would go on to establish and build multiple nonprofits, along with several businesses that have a great impact on the community, and quite literally, the world.

The first began, in many ways, when Ty was just a child carrying around his pet opossum on his shoulder while riding his bike through the neighborhood. His love for "wild" animals had been birthed. Along with the opossum, Ty would go on, years later, to receive clearance from the federal agencies and adopt four black bears and six tigers. His house had become a zoo, and he was living his dream of caring for wild animals. When he and his wife's first child came along, they agreed that the season had shifted. It was time to find another place for these animals. Ty founded a wildlife sanctuary called "Bluegrass Farms." Today, known as "Tiger's For Tomorrow," it continues to thrive as a permanent place for native and exotic animals, as well as an environmental education learning facility for the nearly 30,000 visitors that come by each year. These animals who need a permanent, secure home receive the highest standard of care.

Ty's adventures didn't stop there. One afternoon, he texted a friend and said, "I want you to come and check out this boat I bought." To his friend's disbelief, this was not merely a boat, but a large ship that could accommodate over sixty people. Ty had purchased the boat so he could launch a ministry that would travel from village to village along the Amazon River in South America to provide food to all the families there. The ministry, which continues to grow and thrive today, is called "Amazon Hope." He also established multiple thrift stores in North Alabama to create revenue for the ministry.

He did all of this while also teaching, coaching, running multiple businesses, traveling to do mission work, and leading his family as a husband and father. It all goes back to his dad, who instilled within him that anything is possible if you're willing to work for it.

Ty and his family

DAD STORIES

A TRUCK STOP IN TEXAS

James Anderson

James with his family

A TRUCK STOP IN TEXAS

James Anderson

James Anderson's parents were separated for much of the first ten years of his life, and he doesn't have many good memories of those days. When he was ten, they formally divorced and his dad moved out of the house.

When James was fifteen years old, he and his mom had a big "falling out" and she told him he had to go to live with his dad. By his own account, James was a "bad kid" and was often in trouble for vandalism and illegal drug use. By the time he was eighteen, he had thirteen traffic violations. When he was pulled over for speeding at the age of eighteen, he knew it meant trouble. When the policeman approached his car, there was a terrible misunderstanding about a weapon, and James was charged with aggravated assault on an officer.

He ended up spending a year in jail, and four years on probation. While incarcerated, James thought about the direction his life was heading and knew deep in his heart that it was time to make some big changes, but he couldn't seem to change directions. The gravity of the cycle was pulling him further and further from the better life he longed for. Upon his release from jail, he continued to make bad decisions. He was unfaithful to his wife and, with an infant now in the picture, he went through a terrible divorce. Things were looking more and more grim. He continued the dreaded cycle that had spiraled through his parents. He couldn't get ahead.

While driving a truck through Texas, he stopped at a truck stop. He was 1000 miles from home but, in what seemed to be a divinely-inspired moment, he bumped into an old buddy from home. His old friend wanted to talk to him about Jesus, and while in conversation, James made a commitment to seek a relationship with Christ. What did he have to lose? Nothing else seemed to be working.

As time went on, things began to truly shift for the first time in his life. He's the first to tell you he hasn't been perfect, but things are nowhere near the way they used to be.

Twenty years have passed since that life-changing moment at the Texas truck stop. James continues to do his best to live a life pleasing to God. God has restored his marriage and he and his wife remarried. They had two more boys together and he has helped raise other children who were in a situation he was all too familiar with - one where they were in desperate need of a father figure in their lives.

By all accounts, James' children have had the benefit of being raised in a loving and stable home where they know they are loved and where they receive good guidance. His story is a message to the world that says, "You're not gonna be perfect. But, start where you are and begin improving. You'll look back in ten years and see a massive difference."

James and Scott after James' interview on the "That's My Dad Podcast."

DAD STORIES

A FATHER TO MANY

Eddie Nichols

Eddie with those he poured much of his life into

A FATHER
TO MANY

Eddie Nichols

Since he was a young man, Eddie Nichols has given his life to investing in young men. He was given an outdated, beat-up house not too far from downtown Gadsden, but didn't have the money to fix up the home or to even connect water or power to the home. Knowing that Eddie was serving the homeless in the community, a church in the area gave him a call. There had been a homeless man who was finding his way into their church, and the leaders were concerned about his hygiene and were hoping Eddie could get him some help. Eddie came and picked up the man, drove him into the woods where the house was located, and showed him around the place. Eddie apologized to the man and said, "I'm so sorry that I don't have any water and power." The man replied, "This right here is the best thing I've had in a long time so don't apologize."

At this moment, Eddie realized that you don't have to give "big stuff" to those in need. You just have to show them that you care. This moment was just the beginning of several decades of pouring his life into those who needed help.

He spent many years leading a large, well-known youth ministry - "Breakaway Ministries." Since 1987, they've hosted dozens of youth camps where young men and women from all over the Southeastern United States gather and hear the Gospel of Jesus. The insurmountable impact of "Breakaway Ministries" will only be known in eternity.

Ten years ago, Eddie founded "The Dream Center" - a ministry that was birthed out of a Bible study with a group of young men. In 2012, Eddie hosted this Bible Study with gang members and fatherless children. Only two of the twenty-eightguys had a father in their home. He recalls that one time, one of the guys even stole from the pizza man who was dropping the pizza off. He was often asked, "What's an ole white guy doing with a bunch of gang members?" He wasn't sure, but even in the midst of these types of issues, Eddie kept his eyes locked on the hope of these kids changing course. Many did.

He ran into one of them in Walmart just recently and was greeted with a big hug, a smile, and a "Hey, Mr. Eddie!" The young man was on the phone with his girlfriend and began to tell her about the impact he had on his life. This one example is only a small glimpse into the true impact he's had on so many.

Today, "The Dream Center" is located right in the middle of a community that needs hope. Through their after-school program, mentorship program, and special events, they aim to impact that very community and "eventually change this city by investing in the life of a child."

Eddie's life is a beautiful message to those who are a father to the fatherless. Don't give up on them. When they see that you believe in them, they'll start believing in themselves.

Eddie and his daughter

Eddie and his two sons

Eddie and his wife

DAD STORIES

THROWING BALL WITH DAD

Brian and his dad

THROWING BALL WITH DAD

Brian Mintz

It's the little things. Ever heard that phrase? Well, it's true.

It's true in Brian Mintz's life, as well. As he puts it, it's "the significance of the insignificant."

When Brian was asked about the moments that stand out most to him, it wasn't the extravagant things that parents often feel like they need to do. It was the small moments. It was the time he and his dad went bream fishing. It was the times they were throwing the ball in the backyard. It was the time his dad paid $500 for an old car, and they got to fix it up together. It was the times that they were just together.

This is a beautiful, challenging reminder to all dads that it's not as complicated as we make it. Spend time together.

DAD STORIES

BURGER KING AND ALABAMA FOOTBALL

Mike and his dad, Coy

BURGER KING AND ALABAMA FOOTBALL

Mike Davis

Many families have traditions. There may not be one more special than the one between Mike Davis and his dad.

Mike and his 92-year-old dad, Coy, have always had a close, thriving relationship. He has the utmost respect, honor, and appreciation for the man who sacrificed so much for him. For many years, one of many things they have shared together is their love for Alabama football.

Some traditions are profound and complex while others are simple and seemingly insignificant. Regardless, traditions are often treasured, which is the case with Mike and his dad. It's a tradition that they each look forward to every weekend.

On Saturdays in the fall, on his way to his dad's house to watch the Alabama game, Mike picks up their go-to meal from Burger King. Together, they'll eat their meal and watch the Alabama football game.

Yep, that's it. Maybe you were expecting something jaw-dropping or profound. But, that's not the case here. However, the joy they experience together from doing something so simple is a message the world needs to hear.

DAD STORIES

NEVER CALL ME AGAIN

> Due to the nature of Barry's upbringing, we've changed his name and have not included any photos of him.

NEVER CALL ME AGAIN

Anonymous Guest

Barry's upbringing was traumatic in every sense of the word. It involved some dangerous circumstances he couldn't go into detail about, so to protect him, we've concealed his identity and changed his name.

Barry's father was a member of a notorious motorcycle gang. When Barry was young, his dad abandoned him. It wasn't until his dad had a horrific motorcycle crash that they were forced to reunite because of his dad's need for assistance, but even then, he never became a real dad to Barry. The many years of abuse, neglect, and abandonment had taken their toll. For many years, they didn't even speak to each other.

To make matters even worse, Barry's mother was a drug dealer and was abusing them herself. This lifestyle was all Barry knew. For a season, Barry was pulled into the same generational cycle and began abusing drugs. It looked like the cycle was going to continue through another generation.

Just as life was looking grim, Barry was thrown a lifeline, one that would quite literally shift the course of his family tree. He and his now wife had gotten married and, when they did, his father-in-law stepped in to take Barry under his wing. He would become the man Barry so desperately needed. He poured into him, gave him wisdom, taught him how to be an honorable man, and became like the dad he never had. This is the season that shifted the trajectory of his life.

When Barry was asked what he'd say to his dad today, he responded authentically and vulnerably: "Never call me again."

Sadly, this is reality. If you treat your kids with cruelty for years on end, this is what you get. They don't want anything to do with you.

Although Barry has moved forward from his traumatic past, it's still excruciating to revisit. He was kind enough to tell his story in hopes that it will bring encouragement to a young man who may now be walking in the shoes he once walked in.

Today, Barry has found a way to become an incredible dad to his daughter. He flipped the script. He turned it around.

Due to the nature of Barry's upbringing, we've changed his name and have not included any photos of him.

DAD STORIES

THE POWER OF ADOPTION

Rene, his wife, and their family

THE POWER OF ADOPTION

Rene Zeringue

Rene recalls a time when he was eight, his brother, Kaleb, was seven, and his parents also had four foster children under the age of six. They chose to foster these children who had been raised in difficult circumstances, even though they didn't have to. At one point, they told the fostering agency, "Hey, if you need a place for another child, send them here."

Rene, although he was only a young boy at the time, was being exposed to something special that would make a huge impact in his life not too many years later.

When Rene married his wife, their lives quickly spiraled into an unforeseen direction. They were attending the funeral of one of his wife's family members. When they walked in, sitting on the lap of the widowed father were two five-year-old boys, who were now tragically without their mother. In passing, Rene and his wife compassionately mentioned to the father that they were available to help however he needed them.

The next day, Rene got a phone call from the father who made it clear that he was not going to be able to take care of his two boys. Rene and his wife agreed to take them in temporarily and would take them to see their dad on the weekends.

A few months later, tragically, the boys' dad passed away. Now, their father and their mother had passed. After many conversations, Rene and his wife chose to adopt the boys. Today, they have been married for ten years and they have three biological children and two adopted children - fifteen, fourteen, seven, four, and a baby.

When asked what the best thing about being a dad is, Rene said:
"At this stage of my life, I work more than I ever have. Different schools, different schedules, baby coming, I don't have time for hobbies like I used to. We are a month away from not sleeping anymore and that whole season. When I was single, I got to do all of the things that are supposed to make you happy. I got to sleep full hours of the night, had time for hobbies, and had more money to spend on myself. Incredibly, I wouldn't go back for anything."

Today, he is the Pastor of Ohatchee Church of Christ in Ohatchee, Alabama. He's coached high school football for many years and taught Bible classes at a local Christian School. Rene, who saw his parents' example as a young boy, has now become a man much like his father - selfless, committed, and sacrificial - not only to his kids, but dozens of others.

Rene and his wife

DAD STORIES

TURNING DOWN THE OPPORTUNITY OF A LIFETIME

Taylor Gallman after he told the story of his dad, Andy, on the "That's My Dad Podcast"

61

TURNING DOWN THE OPPORTUNITY OF A LIFETIME

Taylor Gallman

Taylor Gallman's dad, Andy, was a minister who had a big heart to reach young people. In Hattiesburg, Mississippi, Andy was leading a vibrant youth ministry where over 1,500 young people would gather in a stadium every week to hear Andy preach. A group of men who were leaders of a renowned global ministry heard about the impact Andy was having and wanted to syndicate him into full-time ministry, where he would travel the world and preach at their highly-attended events. Andy asked them if he would be required to move. When they told him that he would, he turned down the opportunity of a lifetime, not wanting to uproot his family.

After Andy kindly passed on their offer, they approached another man. Before the young man answered the same question, he asked the group of men, "Was I your first choice?" They replied, "No, sir. Andy Gallman was." He said, "The only way I'll accept is if Andy can be the one who prays for me before each of these events." After agreeing, the young man was quickly thrust into global evangelism where, before each event, he would hop on the phone with Andy Gallman and have him pray over him. That young man would go on to reach hundreds of millions of people.

The moral of the story is not that Andy Gallman could have gone on to achieve great success and become one of the most well-known evangelists to ever live. It's that a young father was willing to turn down the opportunity of a lifetime to stay present with his family and remain planted in the place they had grown to love.

DAD STORIES

Todd and his family

DAD KISSED MOM!

Todd Walker

Todd Walker grew up in a great home with a loving family. He will be the first to tell you that his parents modeled what marriage and family should look like. Even as a young boy, Todd was an observer. He watched the way his dad interacted with his mom - observations that would pay dividends when he became a father.

When Todd was young, each day in the evening when his dad walked through the door after a long day of work, he would go straight to his mom and give her a kiss. For years, it happened the same way, time and time again. This simple act began to stand out to him and was a moment he looked forward to every evening. He wouldn't fully understand the impact of these thousands of moments until later in life.

Seeing this authentic, affectionate moment take place like clockwork, Todd quickly gained a sense of security. Each night, he slept well knowing his Mom and Dad were there to stay. There was a sense of stability that he experienced throughout his childhood. He never had to worry about one of them walking out because he saw with his own eyes how much his parents loved each other. His parents even had their marriage certificate framed and mounted on the wall in their bedroom - a symbol that would remind them and Todd of their commitment to each other.

Today, Todd is following in his dad's footsteps. He gives his own kids immense security by loving and respecting their mother. He considers it one of the greatest joys of his life to serve his family.

DAD STORIES

WHEN I FOUND OUT I WAS GONNA BE A DAD

David with Scott after his episode on the "That's My Dad Podcast"

WHEN I FOUND OUT I WAS GONNA BE A DAD

David Williams

David Williams has always been a gifted athlete. In middle and high school, he achieved great success in multiple sports. While David was getting ready for one of his high school basketball games, in a moment that would change his life, David found out he was going to be a father.

After he confirmed it was true, he did something that shocked everyone. Immediately following that night's game, David stepped away from basketball. He then secured a job, where he'd spend each afternoon and evening working hard to provide for the baby that would soon arrive. As an eighteen-year-old, he stepped up to the plate and made a commitment that his child would never be without clothing, food, shelter, or emotional support.

He had no idea at the time, but he'd need to work extra hard as there wasn't just one baby, but two. He was a father to twins.

David's fierce commitment didn't stop with just a job. After the twins were born, the legal system stepped in to set guidelines for child support. While the judge was determining what his child support requirement would be, David stood and said, "Judge, you can put whatever you want on that paper but know that I'm going to go above and beyond to be sure those children have what they need."

David's commitment still rings true today as, nearly three decades later, he remains unwaveringly committed to four children, who have never seen a day of lack. David continues to be the standard for what a father should be.

THE that's my DAD PROJECT

VISTA McDUFFIE

THE that's my DAD PROJECT

FULL EPISODES

You can watch each of the full episodes on our YouTube Channel.

That's My Dad Project

FATHERHOOD
DOCUMENTARY

Our team put this film together to convey the heart of the "That's My Dad Project" and to tell the inspiring stories of Season 1 of our podcast. Our prayer is that it breaks cycles of generational fatherlessness and inspires fathers to become great dads.

SOCIAL

over 3 million views
across all platforms

YOUTUBE
That's My Dad Project

TIKTOK
@thatsmydad.podcast

FACEBOOK
That's My Dad Project

INSTAGRAM
@thatsmydad.podcast

THE that's my DAD PROJECT

www.ingramcontent.com/pod-product-compliance
Lightning Source LLC
Chambersburg PA
CBHW061357010526
44107CB00012B/959